PSYCHOLOGY
50 KEY IDEAS UNPACKED

PSYCHOLOGY
50 KEY IDEAS UNPACKED

EMILY RALLS & TOM COLLINS

This edition published in 2023 by Arcturus Publishing Limited
26/27 Bickels Yard, 151–153 Bermondsey Street,
London SE1 3HA

AD011247UK

Printed in the UK

Contents

Introduction

We are all psychologists to some extent. We watch those around us and use what we observe to identify the intentions of others. We use evidence from our past to make judgements about our future behaviour. This is, in essence, psychology. It is the systematic study of who we are, how we think and what influences our behaviour. It is the study of us, and we do it unconsciously all the time. But as with other sciences that allow us to study ourselves, such as biology, there are tools and techniques that scientists have developed over time to deepen our understanding.

The different approaches in the study of psychology vary hugely. They can be subjective or scientific, holistic or reductionist, focusing on the traits we share or on individual differences. They have evolved over time and are subject to the trends and politics of their time.

In this book, we present 50 key concepts that provide a summary of psychology. We cover as many philosophies, research methods and approaches as we can to give you an overview of this broad area of study.

It would be impossible to pinpoint when people began thinking about thinking. Psychology, or 'mental philosophy' as it was known until the middle of the 19th century, has taken many forms throughout human history. Classical philosophers such as Plato and Aristotle certainly theorized about the mind as far back as the 5th century BCE, and believed that the mind or soul was a separate entity to the physical body. This approach became known as 'dualism' in the 17th century, when the French philosopher René Decartes theorized that the mind and body communicated only through a small structure in the base of the brain called the pineal gland.

Dualism continued to be the predominant belief until English philosophers Thomas Hobbes and John Locke argued instead that our mental experiences are in fact physical processes that occur within the brain. This approach became known as 'monism'.

However, these philosophical approaches to the mind are not what we would think of as psychology today, and it was not until the 19th century that psychology began to be studied in a scientific and objective way. Modern psychology takes more of a mechanistic approach, considering the mind as a by-product of our physical body.

One big hurdle that had to be overcome in order to reach this stage was working out how to study the mind, something we cannot see or directly observe, and link it to the physical body. Nineteenth-century physiologist Wilhelm Wundt's approach to introspection is what helped bridge this divide, so this is where we will begin.

1

Introspection

Introspection is a process of examining your own thoughts, feelings, actions, even motivations, and using this insight to gain a deeper understanding of the workings of the mind. Introspection is a subjective and individual experience. It was used by Wilhelm Wundt, the founding father of experimental psychology, in his attempts to move the study of the mind away from the subjective self-observation of Wolff and Kant, and establish psychology as an observable science.

WILHELM WUNDT

Although he spent much of his career studying medicine, Wilhelm Wundt (1832–1920) is credited as being the first person to refer to himself as a psychologist. In 1874, he published his groundbreaking book *Principles of Physiological Psychology*, a publication that grew from one 870-page book to three volumes by the time it reached its sixth and final edition in 1908.

Although much of his book concerns physiology, Wundt did not approach psychology from an entirely physiological perspective. He stated that the human mind cannot gather experiences without at the same time speculating on those experiences. It was the first systematic study of the relationship between physiology and psychology, and in the first line of his author's preface Wundt wrote: 'The work which I here present to the public is an attempt to mark out a new domain of science.' This it certainly did.

Wilhelm Wundt is credited with opening the first psychological laboratory in 1879.

EXPERIMENTAL PSYCHOLOGY

Wundt attempted to move away from the concept of dualism that had been so predominant in the study of the mind until this point, and to unify the mind and the body. While he acknowledged the work of his philosophical peers, most notably Wolff and Kant, he rejects their protests that the mind and inner human experience are inaccessible, entirely subjective, and cannot be studied and investigated scientifically.

Previously the mind had mainly been studied using subjective self-observation: essentially, philosophers thinking about thinking using their own observations of human behaviour. It sounds as if Wundt is suggesting that this method of reasoning is flawed, even arrogant, when he outlines that its proponents think that they can 'arrive directly, without further assistance, at an exact characterization of mental facts'. How can an observer observe themself and know that their observation is correct? He wanted to show that by objectively studying the senses, which represent our method of interacting with the world, we can gain a deeper understanding of the mind that is linked to them.

Wundt also felt that the arguments his peers had against the more scientific approach of experimental psychology – that it rejected the idea of introspection – was based on a misunderstanding. Experimental psychology sought to move away from self-observation and to study the mind and introspective processes systematically, using objective, carefully controlled, repeatable observations. He outlines in *Principles of Physiological Psychology* that the aim of experimental procedures in studying introspection is to substitute the subjective method, 'whose sole resource is an inaccurate inner perception', with a method that brings consciousness under 'accurately adjustable objective conditions'.

Wundt believed that experimental psychology shared many characteristics with other scientific disciplines, particularly physics and physiology, even pointing out that they may use many of the same instruments to measure factors such as time. His approach tried to separate the study of the mind from philosophy, and ground it in this new discipline of experimental psychology.

THE FIRST PSYCHOLOGICAL LABORATORY

In 1879, Wundt set up the first psychological laboratory. It was called the Institute for Experimental Psychology, housed in the University of Leipzig, Germany. Here, he attempted to study psychology as any other physical science. He used trained and practised observers and encouraged his

Leipzig's university hall, built in 2008.

students to employ procedures that were carefully controlled, in order to produce the same experience each time. This meant that observations could be repeated and compared, and thus psychology began to take a step away from subjective philosophy.

Wundt argued that we can use external stimuli to modify consciousness, calling this 'modification from without'. We can subject our mental processes to arbitrarily determined conditions, over which we have complete control, and which we may keep constant or vary as we will. An example would be a simple sound or flashing light. Next, we can systematically study our reaction to that stimulus through the process of introspection. Wundt aimed to study psychology with the same rigour and science as other physical sciences, applying systematic techniques.

At the institute, for instance, researchers would expose participants to a ticking metronome or a flickering light and ask them to report the sensations they were feeling. The researcher might observe from a separate room to ensure they had no influence on the results. Early investigations concerned the relationships of simple sensations and perceptions of space and time. Later, researchers began investigating more complex concepts, such as attention, memory and feelings.

The first investigation completed at the institute was conducted by Dr Max Friedrich and titled 'On the duration of apperception in connection with simple and compound sensations'. This was one of many investigations that measured the time taken for certain psychological processes to occur. These processes included reaction time or memory recall, measured precisely and empirically using a piece of equipment called a chronoscope, which could measure reaction speeds to 1/1,000th of a second.

Wundt's obsession with precision and efforts to establish a scientific and systematic study of psychology had limitations. He admitted that other techniques would be necessary to create a comprehensive study of the mind. He also recognized that psychology was an evolving discipline, and communicated this with eloquent modesty in his first book: 'A first attempt, such as this book represents, must show many imperfections; but the more imperfect it is, the more effectively will it call for improvement.' Despite its limitations, the lasting contribution that Wundt's work has made means that many regard him as the father of psychology as a discipline in its own right.

The role of cognitive bias and skill in fruit machine gambling (Griffiths, 1994)

Introspection was one of the earliest methods used to study psychology and is still used now.

One example is from a study by Griffiths (1994), who believed that irrational thought processes were linked to gambling behaviour. He investigated this by comparing participants who gambled regularly with participants who gambled only occasionally. Each was given £3 to gamble on a fruit machine, and half were asked to think aloud while they did so.

Like Wundt, Griffiths' procedures were repeatable because he ensured not only that the process of gambling remained the same for each participant, but that the instructions they were given were also standardized. Each participant was told the same thing:

'The thinking aloud method consists of verbalizing every thought that passes through your mind while you are playing. It is important to remember the following points: 1) Say everything that goes through your mind. Do not censor any of your thoughts even if they seem irrelevant to you. 2) Keep talking *as continuously as possible, even if your ideas are not clearly structured. 3) Speak clearly. 4) Do not hesitate to use fragmented sentences if necessary. Do not worry about speaking in complete sentences. 5) Do not try to justify your thoughts.'*

Whast Griffiths found through this introspective method was that regular gamblers did indeed use more irrational verbalizations: 14 per cent of the regular gamblers made statements such as 'The machine likes me', while only 2.5 per cent of the non-regular gamblers did the same, instead making more rational verbalizations such as 'I lost the whole pound there'.

2
Structuralism

Wilhelm Wundt's scientific approach to the examination of human consciousness became known as 'structuralism'. The structuralist approach attempted to understand the mind as a product of the thoughts and sensations we experience. While Wundt established the founding principles of structuralism, it was his student Edward Bradford Titchener (1867–1927) who is credited with establishing it as a school of thought in psychology.

EDWARD B. TITCHENER

As one of Wundt's students, Edward Bradford Titchener would expand upon Wundt's ideas to found the theory of structuralism. Titchener was born in 1867 in Chichester, England and attended Malvern College on a scholarship. While his family planned for him to enter the clergy, Titchener's focus was on pursuing his interests in science. In 1885, he began studying biology but later went on to study comparative psychology at Oxford. During his time at Oxford, Titchener began to read the work of Wilhelm Wundt and later translated the first volume of Wundt's *Principles of Physiological Psychology* from German into English.

Titchener graduated from Oxford in 1890 and, unable to find work or further study in the UK, he began studying with Wundt in Leipzig, Germany. He would go on to earn his PhD in psychology from the University of Leipzig in 1892. Titchener then took a position as a professor of psychology at Cornell University in New York. It was here that he established the psychological school of thought called structuralism and brought the study of psychology to the USA.

TITCHENER'S INTROSPECTION

Titchener expanded on Wundt's methods by putting his students through an arduous process to become skilled at trained introspection. By looking

Did you see more than just the blue bird? Titchener trained his students to describe in much greater detail what they were experiencing, breaking their observation down into specific elements.

inwardly, students would single out and report only the sensations as they experienced them.

An effective introspectionist would be able to describe the intensity and clarity of the sensations when viewing an image. For example, when looking at an image of a bird a casual observer could just describe it as 'blue'. However, Titchener trained his students to look beyond what their initial attention had been drawn to. Instead, they would be able to describe other elements, such as the tone of blue or the sensation of seeing the bird.

Titchener and his students began analyzing the elements that made up conscious thought. Titchener drew upon his earlier experience in biology and sought to compile a periodic table of these psychological elements using the introspective observations of his students. They examined the laws governing the elements of conscious experience and the connections between sensations. Using these methods, Titchener's students reported on the different elements they experienced and in *An Outline of Psychology* (1899), he reported more than 44,000 elements of sensation.

Titchener concluded that there were three essential elements that made up all conscious experiences: feelings, sensations and images. As his research matured, it also became more limited in its application.

Elementary sensations	Number
Colour	About 35,000
White to black range	600–700
Tones	About 11,000
Tastes	4 (sweet, sour, bitter, salty)
From the skin	4 (pressure, pain, warmth, cold)
From the internal organs	4 (pressure, pain, warmth, cold)
Smells	9 classes seem likely, but there might be thousands of elements
Total elementary sensations	44,000, plus an indeterminate variety of smells

Titchener was aiming to discover how sensations input information into our consciousness and believed it is the elements that he identified that construct the human experience. However, despite their training, Titchener was relying on the subjective views of his students, which ultimately relied on their own conscious experience of the sensations they described. Thus, by modern standards, the structuralist methodology was flawed.

FUNCTIONALISM
Emerging from the structuralist school of thought came 'functionalism'. Psychologists following this school of thought were more interested in the function of each behaviour and how many different behaviours contributed to the success of an organism than in studying each behaviour or sensation individually. William James, the founder of this approach, was first inspired by the writing of Charles Darwin and the concept that our behaviours and characteristics were adaptive, meaning that they served some function to help us survive.

Functionalism differed from its predecessor structuralism in that its proponents sought to investigate how factors worked together to influence behaviour, rather than studying them individually. They also worked towards using more objective techniques in the study of behaviour, and moved away from introspection as a technique of study.

As a movement in psychology, structuralism did not survive much beyond Titchener's death in 1927, when, along with functionalism, it was being overtaken by new schools of thought such as the 'Gestalt movement'. However, the legacy of Titchener's work was to firmly set the stage for psychology to be treated as a scientific enterprise.

3
Gestalt Psychology

Gestalt psychology emerged in Germany in the 20th century in response to functionalism and structuralism. Gestalt theory emphasizes that the whole of anything is greater than its parts, and provided the foundation for the modern study of perception.

PHI PHENOMENON

A simple observation by psychologist Max Wertheimer (1880–1943) became the foundation of Gestalt psychology. Wertheimer's paper 'Experimental Studies of the Perception of Movement' was concerned with optical illusion and human perception of movement. He noted that we can see motion or movement when no actual movement takes place. For example, when we are presented with a series of still images that flash past our eyes very quickly, we can perceive this as being a moving image. Legend has it that Wertheimer made his novel observation while playing with a child's toy on a train during the summer of 1910. He would go on to call this the 'phi phenomenon' (1912). Wertheimer's classic phi phenomenon experiment used slits of light in a revolving tachistoscope wheel to produce a perception of apparent motion.

What is your perception of reality? Do you see a vase or two faces? Max Wertheimer began investigating illusion and the perception of reality in 1912.

A zoetrope works on a principle of apparent movement. Each image is distinctly different, but when shown quickly in sequence gives the impression of movement.

The phi phenomenon was impossible to explain using a structuralist framework, whereby every elementary sensation would be isolated to examine the human experience. Gestalt psychology argued that this apparent movement could not be reduced to individual sensory elements. As the motion is observed, the individual's nervous system does not process the input – the images in this case – in a piecemeal way, but rather assimilates it through many sensory experiences simultaneously. Thus, the visual input springs immediately into existence in the mind as an entire moving image. We are tricked into seeing fluid movement where there is none.

Gestalt, meaning 'form' or 'entire figure' in German (there is no direct translation in English), therefore considers the whole or unity of movement to be of greater importance than the sum of all the individual elements. In later writings, this principle was stated as the 'law of Prägnanz'.

The mechanics of apparent movement were already known prior to Wertheimer's observations. In fact, it had been used in practical applications for more than 60 years in the film industry, and many of its properties seemed to have been worked out before Wertheimer published his paper.

Ray Harryhausen used 1/24th second-per-frame stop animation to simulate apparent movement, a special effect the film industry had been using 60 years before Wertheimer published his theory of phi phenomenon.

WOLFGANG KÖHLER

Perhaps the best known of the Gestalt psychologists was Wolfgang Köhler (1887–1967). He applied the concept of Gestalt far beyond the limit of sensory experience to study problem-solving in apes.

In the Tenerife Island experiments with apes during World War I Köhler observed apes overcoming obstacles to reach a goal object. In a series of experiments, food was placed out of reach behind barriers or through a maze. Earlier experiments with cats and dogs had shown that these animals used trial and error to gain access to the food. Initially, the chimps tried to jump and reach some bananas that had been placed out of reach, becoming frustrated and angry as they failed. Eventually, they used the toys and objects in the enclosure in order to problem-solve and reach the food. Some of the chimps stacked boxes and another, Sulton, was observed to join two short sticks together to make a longer pole that could be used to reach a banana.

The ape's ability to problem-solve by insight and seeing relationships between objects and stimuli supported the assumptions of the Gestalt approach: that behaviour cannot be explained by examining individual sensory responses, but requires an understanding of multiple factors that may be interacting.

Wertheimer, Köhler, Kurt Koffka (1886–1941) and their students extended the Gestalt approach to problems in other areas of perception, problem-solving, learning and thinking: Gestalt principles were later applied to motivation, social psychology and personality.

GESTALT THERAPY

By the 1940s, the founders of the Gestalt movement had fled the Nazi regime of Germany and brought their influence to the USA, where a psychotherapeutic approach developed by Friedrich S. Perls (1893–1970) and others emerged.

Although not directly connected to the original ideals of Gestalt, this branch of therapy takes into account the whole individual and is concerned with the obstacles to the functioning of the whole person in the context of the present. In other words, Gestalt therapy emphasizes the present moment and personal responsibility.

The practice uses cognitive insight into current experiences, and emphasizes mindfulness, encouraging the person being treated to explore creativity to achieve satisfaction in areas of life that may have otherwise been blocked. The basis of this approach to therapy is self-awareness

Sulton joining two sticks together in order to reach the bananas, whereas Grande has decided to try a more perilous tactic of stacking boxes to retrieve the food.

of behaviour, emotion, feelings, perception and sensation in order to understand the whole. In 1951, Perls produced the book *Gestalt Therapy: Excitement and Growth in the Human Personality,* based mostly on his own research and clinical notes. Shortly after the publication in 1951, Perls founded the New York Institute for Gestalt Therapy and began to train therapists in his principles.

Although it did not survive as a distinct school of psychology much beyond the 1950s, Gestalt psychology made an important contribution to understanding how reality is perceived. From the early experiments into illusion and problem-solving experiments in apes, Gestalt psychology has shown us that the perception of the whole may be greater than the sum of all parts that construct our reality.

4

Perception

What can you see in the picture below? If you are not familiar with the image you will just see a collection of black and white blotches. However, many people will be able to pick out the image of a Dalmatian dog. What is striking about this image is that there is no outline of a Dalmatian. Our mind merely perceives the shapes it recognizes as a Dalmatian sniffing at the ground as it walks away, and fills in the missing information for us.

VISUAL PERCEPTION

We tend to organize visual information so that we see patterns. In Chapter 2, we discussed how the research by Edward B. Titchener identified around 46,708 elementary senses, and how he believed that conscious experience could be understood from the input of these senses to the brain. The Gestalt school of thought, by contrast, posited that we create a perception of our reality as a whole rather than the sum of all the parts.

A Dalmatian dog appears from a collection of individually uninterpretable blotches. From James (1965).

The five senses

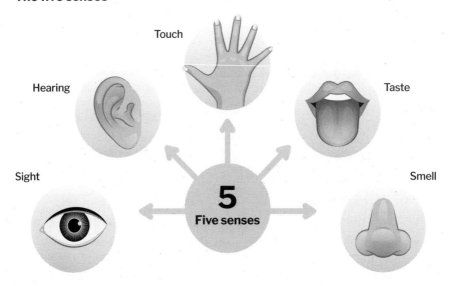

There is a similar debate about how we receive and organize visual information. The 'bottom-up' argument suggests that our perceptions are based entirely on the information received by our eyes. The alternative 'top-down' approach suggests that in order to make sense of the huge amount of data we are receiving, our mind creates an expectation of what we are perceiving and fits the information into this preconception.

In 1970, psychologist Richard Gregory (1923–2010) believed that perception is a constructive procedure. We combine direct visual data received by the eye with stored knowledge in our mind, and construct images that way. He argued that perception is based on three aspects:

1. Sensory data from our surroundings.
2. Memories of past experiences.
3. A hypothesis and inferences that our mind constructs.

We need either cognitive information from past experiences or stored knowledge to help us understand what our eyes are showing us because the data we receive through our senses is frequently ambiguous and sometimes conflicting.

A good example of this is the Necker cube (overleaf). If you stare at the image and focus on the crosses, the cube can 'flip' and change orientation. If you continue to stare at the cube, the image will become unstable and can produce two perceptions, flipping back and forth between the orientations. Gregory thought that this occurred because the brain develops two hypotheses that are equally plausible but cannot decide which to accept.

Therefore, the changes in perception cannot be due to bottom-up processing as the visual input has not changed. The changes must then result from a top-down 'misapplied' hypothesis from the brain of what is near and what appears to be further away.

Gregory also demonstrated this effect of perception with a hollow mask of a face. When we look at a concave mask it is almost impossible not to see it as convex. This is because the stored knowledge of reality we hold in our mind means that we have a tendency to 'see faces', and this overrides the information about depth perception that we are receiving from our senses. This phenomenon can also explain why people often see a face on the Moon.

For Gregory, perception is a hypothesis that our mind constructs. The brain must make inferences about the external environment based on prior knowledge. In this way, we are actively constructing our own perception of reality based on an amalgamation of information supplied by the senses and information stored in memory. However, this theory is

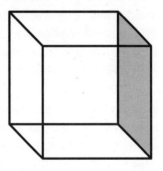

A Necker cube can create a visual illusion whereby the orientation of the cube appears to flip. Gregory argued this was due to a conflicting hypothesis in the mind between sensory input and what you expect to see.

Is this person looking directly at you, or facing to the side? This is an example of our perceptions in conflict.

A concave carving of a face. However, because your mind expects to see a protruding face, you may be able to perceive a convex carving as well.

mostly based on illusions observed in artificial settings. In a real-world setting, there are other senses that complement sight that serve to correct any misconceptions.

GIBSON'S FIELD THEORY

In 1996, James Gibson (1904–79) disagreed with Gregory's concept that our perception is merely a hypothesis of our mind, and instead proposed that perception results from direct information from our senses. Gibson developed his theory of direct perception from his work during World War II training pilots to land aircraft. He determined that all a pilot needed to land an aircraft was the horizon line, runway outline, ground texture and apparent movement of the land. In this sense, the information we receive from the environment is enough to solely construct our perception of reality. What you see is what you get.

Gibson referred to the mechanism for interpreting visual input as the 'optic array'. As we move through our environment, objects directly in front appear stationary, representing a fixed point, but objects to the side appear to move towards us, creating an optic flow (page 27).

Changes in the optic flow give us important clues about the environment. As incoming light rays reflecting off surfaces enter the eye, the apparent brightness of an object as well as its size can indicate how far away it is. Other clues, such as a closer object blocking the image of one that is further away, aid perception. As you move through the visual environment, these aspects will change relative to your location.

Gibson also thought that there are some aspects ('invariants') that do not change, and that these are equally important for accurate perception. Most objects have a visual texture, but this varies depending on how close or far away the object is. When we move away from the object, the grain appears to become finer and as we move towards an object, the texture density becomes coarse. By this means, we are able to judge our distance to the object. So, as the observer moves around their environment, features of the environment change.

Perspective and horizon-ratio relation is another example of an invariant feature in visual perception. Our point of focus has a vanishing point on the horizon where lines of perspective converge. We would see this if we were to look at a set of railway tracks disappearing into the distance. Using these background visual clues we can judge the size of an object or how far away it is. However, this can cause objects that are different sizes to appear to be the same size, since their horizon ratio is the same. Gibson argued that this effect was therefore created by sensory input rather than stored perceptions. A fun example of this phenomenon is the Ames room illusion, which uses this effect to change the apparent size of people in a room.

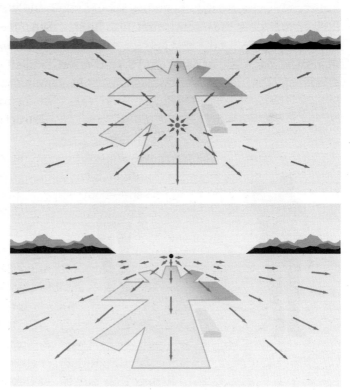

How the optic flow changes for a pilot a) coming in to land and b) flying over an airfield.

27

THE AIR NEW ZEALAND 901 DISASTER

On 28 November 1979, Air New Zealand Flight 901 took off from Auckland Airport. The 237 passengers and 20 crew were on a sightseeing flight to Antarctica. The plane would make several circuits over McMurdo Sound, a relatively low, flat area of ice and frozen water, so that the tourists could take photos and look at the volcanoes and mountains in the distance. However, the flight path that was entered into the plane's computer was different to the one the pilots had been briefed on. Instead of McMurdo Sound, the aircraft headed across Ross Island, and toward the 3,794 m (12,448 ft) volcano Mount Erebus.

To give their passengers a better view, pilots regularly flew low over the area, a manoeuvre that was well within the flight restrictions on that clear day. Permission was given for the crew to descend to 3,050 m (10,000 ft) and proceed with the pilots navigating visually, rather than using their navigation system, on a final low-level pass of the continent. As the plane descended into danger, the white of the ice blended with the white of the mountain, a phenomenon known as a 'whiteout'. With no contrast to show the sloping up of the land, the pilots were completely unaware that they were about to fly straight into the side of the mountain, despite it being directly in front of them. The pilots trusted the flight path computer that had led them to this location and relied on their own memories of McMurdo Sound to guide them visually. They

Horizon-ratio relation. The three people shown here are all the same size, but the ratio of horizon lines may cause us to perceive them as being of different heights, with the smallest on the left.

The Ames room illusion makes one person look small because the room is cleverly distorted. Although the floor appears level, it is actually at an incline, making the person on the left large and the person on the right smaller. Seckel and Klarke (1997) suggest this is because of the horizon-ratio relation.

expected to see flat land based on their prior experiences, and so that is what they perceived.

Twelve seconds before the inevitable impact the low-altitude collision alarm sounded. The crew suddenly realized their error, but by now it was too late and the plane's fate was sealed. All 257 passengers and crew on board were killed. The incident remains the worst crash in Air New Zealand's history and shocked the whole nation. At the root of the crash was the reliance on the incorrect flight path and the visual illusion that the pilots had experienced, resulting in them failing to take action early enough to avoid the mountain. Many lessons were learned and systems and pilot training were improved.

A visual illusion known by pilots as 'whiteout' was a major cause of the Air New Zealand Flight 901 crash in 1979. The plane crashed into the side of Mount Erebus (pictured) despite clear weather, as the pilots didn't recognize that what they were seeing was a mountain.

Gibson's theory that we have a direct visual perception of our environment certainly has far-reaching applications, from informing road marking designs and driver safety, through to pilot training. When the viewing situation is clear and unambiguous, Gibson's theory provides a good explanation for perception. However, incidents such as the crash of Flight 901 highlight the role of memory as a formative influence on our visual perception. What we expect to see influences our perception of the real world. Fortunately, illusions such as that experienced by the flight crew of Flight 901 are rare in the real world. However, they do provide evidence for Gregory's theory that our visual perception is a construction of both what we see *and* what we expect to see.

5
Psychodynamic Theory

You will see a bust of Sigmund Freud (1856–1939) in any film set of a psychiatrist's office, his cigar and glasses conjuring images of an Austrian accent questioning you about your relationship with your mother. Although most of his works were written and published in German, he coined phrases that have become part of our everyday language and he even has a social faux pas named after him, the 'Freudian slip'. Freud was the founder of psychodynamic theory.

SIGMUND FREUD

Freud began his scientific career at the University of Vienna Medical School. One of his first courses was 'General Biology and Darwinism', and Freud was certainly influenced by Darwinian concepts, believing that our biology is the 'bedrock' of our psychology and that much of our psychology is the result of our unconscious biological urges and how we manage them, and that this process begins in childhood.

Sigmund Freud was born in Moravia (now a part of the Czech Republic) to Jewish parents. He grew up in Vienna but fled to London in 1933 to escape persecution by the Nazi government.

Carl Jung, founder of analytical psychology.

CARL JUNG

Another noteworthy figure in the history of the psychodynamic approach to psychology is Carl Jung (1875–1961). Jung expanded on Freud's theories to include such concepts as the 'Electra complex'. Jung and Freud worked closely together for several years, with Freud considering Jung his protégé. However, on a lecture tour of America in 1912 Jung publicly criticized Freud's concept of the Oedipus complex, and their relationship was irrevocably damaged.

Jung went on to develop his own branch of psychology: analytical psychology. He had a more philosophical outlook on psychology than Freud and took a spiritual approach in some areas of his work although he considered himself a man of science. Jung proposed, for example, that humans share a collective unconscious: we have innate memories of our ancestral past that influence our behaviour. He called these universal human themes 'archetypes', and used them to explain recurring themes across cultures, such as shared moral values or similarities in folk stories.

THE UNCONSCIOUS MIND

Theories included in the psychodynamic approach are based on the assumption that there are elements of our behaviour led by unconscious mental processes. These can be influenced by our innate biological drives or by our past experiences. For example, events in our childhood, particularly interactions with our parents, shape our adult personality.

Like an iceberg, some of our drives are apparent and appear above the surface in our conscious mind, but a lot of what drives our behaviour lies below the surface. We can investigate these unconscious processes using methods such as free association or dream analysis, but much remains unknown to us.

CRITICISM

Psychodynamic theories remain popular as they can explain the impact of early development on behaviour and personality later in life. They also account for the influence of biology, our innate, unconscious drives, but also our environment, in terms of how interactions during childhood shape who we become. This approach can be criticized for being overly deterministic. If biology and childhood experiences shape who we are, then surely behaviour is predetermined by forces outside of our control?

As much of what is proposed by psychodynamic theory takes place in our unconscious mind, it is very difficult to study. Much psychodynamic theory is unfalsifiable, meaning that no test or experiment can be designed to prove it wrong. Being unable to prove something wrong does not logically dictate that it is or could be correct. In fact, it implies the opposite: it cannot be scrutinized and shown to be correct. Despite these shortcomings, psychodynamic theory continues to influence modern psychology and psychotherapy.

6
Psychosexual Stages

Sigmund Freud proposed that our personality develops in five stages during childhood, called psychosexual stages. We are not conscious of passing through these stages, but how successful we were at negotiating them can be interpreted from our adult behaviours.

LIBIDO AND FIXATION

At each stage, our 'libido', or pleasure-seeking, is expressed by a different part of the body. The libido must be satisfied before we can successfully move on to the next stage and our parents play a large role in supporting us through this. Freud thought that a well-adjusted adult will have passed through these stages easily and resolved any conflicts between the libido and their psyche. However, the more difficult we find it to satisfy the libido and move through a stage, the more that stage will influence our adult behaviour.

Too much or too little stimulation of the libido at each stage can lead to 'fixation' and unhealthy behaviours later in life. For example, the first stage we go through as a baby is the oral stage, where our libido or pleasure-seeking instinct is focused on our mouth and we gain pleasure from sucking, biting and generally putting anything within reach into our mouths, often to the horror of new parents. This oral focus makes biological sense as a baby's main aim is to acquire food from its

The five psychosexual stages of childhood.

parents, and a baby who is not obsessed by suckling is at serious risk of becoming malnourished.

However, if a person becomes fixated at the oral stage (maybe because they were weaned too early or too late) they may be preoccupied with their mouth as an adult. Freud thought that evidence of fixation at the oral stage could include behaviour such as an adult biting their nails, smoking, sucking their thumb or overindulging in food.

Similarly, each stage has signals of fixation that might be evident in an adult, with the exception being the latency stage, during which time the libido is dormant and children can focus their pleasure-seeking energy on learning and developing friendships (see table on page 37).

Psychosexual stages:

Freud suggested that our personality develops in childhood during five stages: oral, anal, phallic, latency and genital.

Libido:

Psychic energy that is associated with instincts, often associated with sexual or pleasure-seeking urges.

THE OEDIPUS COMPLEX

One particularly interesting, and controversial, psychosexual stage is the phallic stage. The focus of the libido at this point is on the phallus, or penis. At this stage, children begin to notice physical differences between the two sexes, and boys are supposed to experience what Freud called the 'Oedipus complex', named after the mythical Greek king.

During the phallic stage, boys unconsciously see their father as a rival and wish to usurp him. At the same time, they focus their pleasure-seeking desires on their mother and wish to possess her. Boys also worry that their father will find out about these feelings and punish them by taking away their most treasured object, which at that time is their penis. This leads to another complex known as 'castration anxiety'. A child successfully passes through this stage by identifying with their same-sex parent and adopting their behaviours, so in boys this will include imitating the male gender role and displaying masculine-type behaviours.

This theory supports a common criticism of Freud, which is that his work often ignores female psychology. In 1963, Carl Jung expanded Freud's theory to include the Electra complex. He proposed that during the phallic stage, girls notice that they are physically different in that they don't have a penis, and that their mother does not have a penis either. They do not develop castration anxiety as boys do, but instead leap to the conclusion that they have already been castrated by their mother. They become jealous and develop penis envy, leading to a sexual attraction to their father and hostility towards their mother.

Once a girl successfully resolves her Electra complex, she represses her rage and accepts that she will live a penis-less life, identifies with her mother, and replaces her wishes to possess a penis with the wish to have a baby.

LITTLE HANS (FREUD, 1909)

Freud's theories surrounding psychosexual stages derive in part from his study of a young boy known as Little Hans. Hans had a phobia of horses and Freud set out to investigate the possible causes. He found that Little Hans had also shown an interest in penises, or 'widdlers' as he called them. Freud theorized that there could be a link between the large penis of a horse and Hans' phobia.

As Hans' phobia improved, he began to only fear horses wearing a black harness on their nose. His father wondered if the harness symbolized a moustache to Hans, and Freud then concluded that Hans' fear of horses might be symbolic of his fear of his moustachioed father.

Linking to his theory of the Oedipus complex, Freud suggested that Hans had or would resolve this unconscious conflict with his father by fantasizing about having a big penis and marrying his mother, allowing him to identify with his father and also overcome his castration anxiety.

CRITICISM

Although Jung has attempted to redress the balance and include an explanation for female sexual development here, he is criticized for assuming that women are defined by their jealousy of male genitals, and propagating a male-centric view of psychological development. This is of course not the only criticism of the concept of psychosexual stages. It is difficult to test Freud's theories as they occur in our unconscious mind, which is inaccessible even by the person whose mind it is. However, these shortcomings do not detract from the role played by these theories in the history of psychology and our understanding of the mind.

Stage	Ages	Focus of libido	Major development	Adult fixation example
Oral	0–1	Mouth, tongue, lips	Weaning off breast feeding or formula	Smoking, overeating
Anal	1–3	Anus	Toilet training	Orderliness, messiness
Phallic	3–6	Genitals	Resolving Oedipus/ Electra complex	Deviancy, sexual dysfunction
Latency	6–12	None	Developing defence mechanisms	None
Genital	12+	Genitals	Reaching full sexual maturity	If all stages were successfully completed then the person should be sexually mature and mentally healthy

7

The Tripartite Mind

As part of the psychodynamic theory, Sigmund Freud proposed that the human mind is split into three parts: the id, the ego and the superego. Each part of this tripartite mind battles to meet its own needs, mostly in our unconscious, and our behaviour is a result of balancing the needs of each part.

THE TRIPARTITE MIND

Each of these three parts of the mind develop at different points in our life, and have different needs and desires that influence our unconscious mind. Freud proposed that the id develops first and is present in newborns. This bit of the tripartite personality is split into two parts, named after figures in Greek mythology: 1) Eros (god of love), focusing on life and sexual instincts; and 2) Thanatos (god of death), which focuses on death instincts.

The id encourages us to seek immediate satisfaction of instinctual biological urges, such as to obtain food or seek pleasurable experiences. We are entirely unaware of its influence over our behaviour as the id acts entirely in our unconscious mind. It is impulsive and pleasure-seeking, which is an advantage to a newborn baby who needs to seek resources from its parents to survive.

The submerged part of the iceberg represents the unconscious mind.

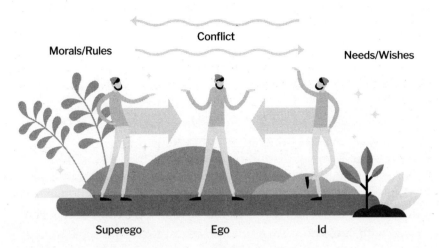

The tripartite personality consists of the id, the ego and the superego.

Freud considered the superego to be the antithesis to the id. It is the angel on our shoulder that counteracts the insatiable, pleasure-seeking demands of the id. The supego develops over time, a result of our interactions with family, friends and society. Like the id, it is split into two parts: 1) the conscience and 2) the ideal self. This ideal self is the benchmark we use to judge ourselves against. If we do not meet the expectations of the ideal self we feel guilt and shame. Although the superego acts largely in our unconscious mind, it differs from the id and can encroach on the conscious mind.

Finally, the ego represents our conscious self. It mediates between the id and the superego to try to meet the demands of the id, while also acting in a socially appropriate way. A strong ego will allow the id and superego to express themselves, but only at appropriate times. If the ego is weak, the id may dominate a person's behaviour, resulting in impulsive and self-destructive behaviour. If the superego dominates a person may become overly self-critical and moralistic, resulting in anxiety disorders and neurosis.

EGO DEFENCE MECHANISMS

Freud believed that the id and superego are in constant conflict in an attempt to influence the ego, and the ego is at risk of becoming overwhelmed by these insatiable demands. To protect itself, the ego uses defence mechanisms. These mechanisms are unconscious – we do not know that the ego is using them – but they can result in psychological abnormalities of their own. If you have heard of someone being 'in denial' about something that has happened to them, this is an ego defence mechanism.

Some of the best known defence mechanisms are denial, repression, regression and projection:

- **Denial**: Refusal to accept that an event or experience has occurred or will occur such as the death of a loved one.
- **Repression**: Keeping disturbing or traumatic thoughts in the unconscious mind and not allowing them into the conscious such as no memory of childhood abuse.
- **Regression**: Behaving as you would have in a previous time when faced with stress now. An adult may revert to irresponsible teenage behaviours when overwhelmingly stressed.
- **Projection**: Attributing your own disturbing thoughts or behaviours to others: if you dislike a person but know this is a socially unacceptable emotion, you may imagine that they in fact do not like you.

8
Dream Analysis

Sigmund Freud called dreams the 'royal road' to the unconscious mind. He believed that they were a way for us to fulfil our unconscious wishes, and could therefore reveal what those unconscious wishes were.

UNCOVERING THE UNCONSCIOUS MIND

Freud did not set out to 'interpret' dreams, but rather to use dreams to uncover unconscious thoughts. The purpose of dream analysis therapy was to uncover the latent meaning of a dream by analyzing the manifest content that was remembered by a patient.

Dream analysis links to other areas in the psychodynamic approach to psychology in the following ways:

- **The tripartite mind**: The id is the source of our wishes and fantasies. In our conscious mind these are deemed unacceptable and suppressed by the ego and superego. They are repressed into our dreams.
- **Defence mechanisms**: Some events or memories are so traumatic we repress them into our unconscious mind. They then only reappear in dreams.

> **Manifest content:**
> What you remember from your dream.
>
> **Latent content:**
> The hidden meaning behind what occurred in your dream.

Freud thought that the desires and fears of our unconscious mind can surface when we are asleep because the ego's defences are lowered. This means that some of the repressed material from our unconscious mind comes through to awareness, albeit in distorted form. He thought that dreams represented unconscious wish fulfilment, and the meaning of these dreams was disguised by symbolism and dreamwork.

WISH FULFILMENT

Freud proposed that unconscious desires (wishes) are repressed by the ego and superego. In 'The Censorship of Dreams' (1915), he gave the following definition: 'Dreams are things which get rid of (psychical) stimuli disturbing to sleep, by the method of hallucinatory satisfaction.' In this case, psychical stimuli might mean a wish or desire in the unconscious mind that has not been satisfied.

SYMBOLISM

If a badger appeared in your dream, what would it mean? A dream interpretation dictionary might suggest that a badger represents victory over opponents or how someone in power is giving you a hard time, or 'badgering' you.

In fact, Freud was very cautious about interpreting symbols in dreams. He did not believe that there were universal symbols, and 'dream dictionaries' were a source of irritation for him. Each symbol will have a different meaning for each person, depending on their life experience, and Freud believed that it was the job of the therapist to identify the latent meaning of the manifest content of a dream by investigating the patient's past.

DREAMWORK

Dreamwork is the process by which the unconscious mind alters the manifest content of dreams in order to conceal their real meaning from the dreamer. Freud believed that our unconscious wishes and desires would be disturbing to our sleep, so dreamwork transforms the forbidden wish into a less threatening form, allowing us to sleep undisturbed by our apparently outrageous desires.

The purpose of dream analysis is to attempt to decode the meaning of a dream, to reverse the dreamwork process. In order to do this, Freud would not attempt to explain the meaning of their dreams to his patients; he would instead use techniques such as free association to encourage his patients to make their own associations between what had appeared in their dream and what unconscious thoughts they represented.

FREUD'S DREAM (Freud, 1895)

On 24 July 1895, Freud had his own dream, which was to form the basis of his theory. He had been worried about a patient, Irma, who was not doing as well in treatment as he had hoped. Freud dreamed that he met Irma at a party and examined her. He then saw a chemical formula for a drug that another doctor had given Irma flash before his eyes and realized that her condition was caused by a dirty syringe. Freud's guilt was thus relieved.

Freud concluded that his dream represented his own unconscious wish fulfilment. He had blamed himself for the fact that Irma was not improving, and was feeling guilty. His unconscious wish was that Irma's poor condition was not his fault and the dream had fulfilled this wish by informing him that another doctor was at fault.

Based on this dream, Freud went on to propose that a major function of dreams was the fulfilment of wishes.

FREE ASSOCIATION

While using free association, a therapist encourages their patient to discuss uncritically the thoughts that come to the forefront of their mind. The therapist might say a word to stimulate the patient's thoughts, and the patient is expected to discuss what they immediately think of. Of course, some patients may be reluctant to discuss the first thing they think of if it is socially unacceptable or traumatic for them, but Freud believed that even long pauses during free association are significant. They can be an indication that the patient is approaching a significant memory or desire.

MODERN APPLICATION

Despite the difficulty of studying the subjective experience of dreams and providing evidence for Freud's theories, dream analysis is still used regularly by therapists. A survey of German psychotherapists in 2000 found that working on dreams is still important in their psychotherapy, with around 28 per cent of sessions involving some form of dream analysis. They also reported that their patients benefited from the technique (Schredl et al., 2000).

9

Humanistic Psychology

Developed in the 1960s and '70s in the USA, the humanistic approach in psychology was a response to the continual tussle between behavioural theorists and cognitive psychologists. The humanistic view was that the study of psychology should focus not just on the impact of the environment on behaviour or the purely mechanistic aspects of cognition, but that the emphasis of psychological study should centre on the human experience.

The roots of humanistic psychology can be found in the existential philosophy that emerged in Europe during the later half of the 19th century. Philosophers attempted to help people come to terms with their often painful existence in the world. In this sense, humanistic psychology is a highly therapeutic approach, as opposed to a purely theoretical one. The goal is to help people deal with life more effectively rather than gaining a total understanding of human behaviour.

MASLOW'S HIERARCHY OF NEEDS

Abraham Maslow (1908–70) was one of the leading theorists in humanistic psychology. Maslow attempted to develop a theory that could explain the range of human needs and motivation.

Maslow is perhaps best known for his hierarchy of needs theory. In this, he proposes that human beings have certain fundamental needs and that these must be met in a particular order. Typically, Maslow's hierarchy of needs is represented as a pyramid, with the most fundamental needs required for survival at the base and the highest level of psychological need, self-actualization, at the top.

Maslow believed that it was vital that each underlying need was met before a person could move up the pyramid to the higher needs, and that

Abraham Maslow was an American psychologist primarily interested in motivation and our innate human need to self-actualize.

this process continued throughout a person's lifetime. He would later clarify that it was not essential for an individual to necessarily meet all of the requirements of each stage in order for them to progress. Maslow also said that the hierarchy could be applied separately to different areas of a person's life, such as a desire to be the best parent they could be.

Maslow studied the personalities of people whom he believed were healthy, creative and productive, in order to better understand what characteristics they possessed that allowed them to achieve self-actualization. These included Eleanor Roosevelt, Albert Einstein, Abraham Lincoln, Thomas Jefferson and others. Maslow believed that self-actualizers were the supreme achievers in the human race and discovered that they shared similar traits, such as being creative, open, spontaneous, loving, compassionate and concerned for others. Additionally, the majority of self-actualizers were rooted in reality, accepting what could not be changed, while at the same time actively tackling problems that could be solved.

They described intense 'peak experiences' where they transcended their own being, giving them a feeling of meaningfulness that they would then repeatedly seek out. Many of these people also interacted in

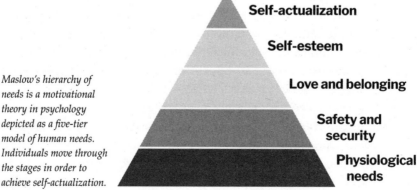

Maslow's hierarchy of needs is a motivational theory in psychology depicted as a five-tier model of human needs. Individuals move through the stages in order to achieve self-actualization.

Self-actualization

Self-esteem

Love and belonging

Safety and security

Physiological needs

small groups with which they maintained healthy relationships. Maslow would go on to say that people who are self-actualized demonstrate a 'coherent personality syndrome' and represent optimal psychological health and functioning.

However, for some, progress is often unfortunately disrupted by a failure to satisfy lower-level needs. Although every person may have the desire to move up the hierarchy, they may fluctuate between the different stages. This could be due to life events such as divorce, loss of income or homelessness. Therefore, not everyone is able to transition through the hierarchy in a singular direction and there may be back-and-forth movement between the stages as a person's needs change throughout their life.

CRITICISMS

Maslow's hierarchy has been criticized for lacking evidence and scientific rigour. The holistic approach and subjective nature of the study means there is potentially a great deal of variation between individuals. Furthermore, it reflects Western values and ideologies, meaning there is no accurate formula to achieve self-actualization that can be universally applied. However, Maslow stretched the field of psychological study beyond only those who had psychoses, to include fully functional individuals, and in doing so he shed a more positive light on personality psychology. Maslow summed up his approach best in his own words, saying: 'It is as if Freud supplied us the sick half of psychology and we must now fill it out with the healthy half.'

CARL ROGERS

Along with Maslow, one of the founding members of the humanist movement was Carl Rogers (1902–87). He was a prominent psychologist and focused on the growth potential of healthy individuals, significantly contributing to our understanding of the self and personality. Both Rogers and Maslow embraced free will and self-determination, believing in the individual's desire to become the best person they could be. Carl Rogers advanced the field of humanistic psychology with his theory of personality development. He devised the term 'actualizing tendency', which describes our basic motive to succeed at our highest possible capacity. He emphasized that the human person is an active, creative, experiencing being who lives in the present, exercising free will and subjectively responding to perceptions of the world around them. Rogers believed that people were

Carl Rogers was a humanistic psychologist who agreed with the main assumptions of Abraham Maslow but added that you needed unconditional love, the correct environment and empathy in order to lead 'the good life'.

inherently good and, like a flower, if the environmental conditions were correct, people would be able to flourish and reach their potential.

He was the first to develop the therapeutic technique of viewing oneself in an unconditional, positive and accepting light, without being unduly critical or harsh. He termed this approach 'unconditional positive regard' and used these techniques to guide his patients to wellness. This 'patient control' was a leap forward in therapeutic approach, and at the time revolutionized the field of humanistic psychology.

IDEAL SELF VS THE REAL SELF

Central to Rogers' theory is that for a person to achieve self-actualization they must have consistency between what he termed the 'ideal self' and the 'real self'. The ideal self is the person whom you would like to be; the real self is the person you actually are. 'Congruence' is where we

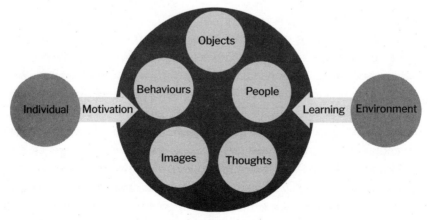

The phenomenal field is the subjective reality drawn from the person's environment and motivations that act on their development of self.

experience similar thoughts about our real self and ideal self and our self-concept is therefore accurate. High congruence is characterized by a greater sense of self-worth and a productive, healthy life. However, when there is a large discrepancy between our real self and ideal self, we experience a state Rogers termed 'incongruence', which can sometimes lead to an inability to cope with the demands of normal life.

THE GOOD LIFE

Rogers thought of life in terms of principles as opposed to stages of development. Rather than static states, he argued that these principles operate in a fluid way. A fully functioning person would continually aim to fulfil their potential. However, this was seen as a continuous and changing process of 'becoming' rather than steps to reach an end goal. This is what Rogers called 'the good life'. 'The good life is a process, not a state of being. It is a direction, not a destination.' (Carl Rogers, 1967)

Rogers identified five similar character traits among people he identified as fully functioning:

1. Openness to experience: A move away from defensiveness, where both positive and negative emotions are accepted and problems are worked through.
2. Existential lifestyle: Fully experiencing events as they occur in the moment, rather than distorting past or future events to fit the self-concept of personality.
3. Trust feelings: Trusting feelings, instincts and gut reactions, believing people's own decisions are the right ones and that they make the right choices.
4. Creativity: There is not a need to conform, and creative thinking and risk-taking are features of a person's life.
5. Rich, full life: A person is always looking for new challenges and experiences and is intensely happy and satisfied with life.

Rogers thought that fully functioning people are well balanced and interesting to know and that such people are high achievers in society.

As with Maslow, Rogers' theories and therapeutic approach had little empirical evidence to support them. Critics would argue that the fully functioning person is a construct of Western culture. In other cultures, the achievement of the group is valued above that of the achievements of any one person.

Overall, the holistic approach of humanism allows for a great deal of insight into the individual. However, there is little empirical evidence to identify enough constant variables for it to be researched with true accuracy and therefore support the key theories. Nevertheless, the approach pushed psychology into new areas, looking at healthy individuals rather than just those who required psychological intervention. In this sense, the humanistic approach broadened the appeal of psychology and gave us all a better understanding of our motivations and what we need to live 'the good life'.

10

The Behavioural Approach

Behaviourists sought to return psychology to a purer, more subjective science than that of psychodynamic theories. A founder of the approach, John B. Watson (1878–1958) stated that: 'The behaviourist cannot find consciousness in the test-tube of his science.' Behaviourists focus on measuring cause and effect. They change a stimulus in the environment of their subject and measure only the responses they can directly observe. They do not seek to explain the processes or cognition that occurs in between.

COMPARATIVE PSYCHOLOGY

Behaviourists believe that humans and non-human animals learn in very similar ways, so by studying animals we can gain insights into human behaviour. Some of the most famous behavioural studies involve the use of animals, for example Pavlov's study of classical conditioning in dogs or Skinner's experiments in the effects of rewards and punishments on pigeons and rats.

Research of this kind began with Edward Thorndike (1874–1949). He studied learning in animals using puzzle boxes. The animal had to pull a lever to escape the box and reach a piece of food. Thorndike observed how long it took the animal, usually a cat, to work out the purpose of the lever. He tested the same animal again and again in the puzzle box and recorded their time in each trial, seeing how their time improved over multiple trials. From these observations, Thorndike developed the law of effect, which states that behaviour will be repeated, or not, based on the effect it has. If the consequences are pleasurable, such as reaching a piece of food, the behaviour will be repeated. If the consequences are not, the behaviour will not be repeated.

> *'Give me a dozen healthy infants, well-formed, and my own specified world to bring them up and I'll guarantee to take any one at random and train him to become any type of specialist I might select – doctor, lawyer, merchant-chief, and yes, even beggarman and thief, regardless of his talents, penchants, tendencies, abilities, vocations, and race of his ancestors.'* John B. Watson, 1924

THE BLANK SLATE

Behaviourists also assume that humans are born with a psychological blank slate that will be written on through experience. Our behaviours are therefore learned through interactions with the environment during our lifetime, often through a process called 'conditioning'. What is proposed by this approach is known as 'environmental determinism', in that our behaviour is determined by our environment. If we assume our behaviour is determined by factors outside of our control, it raises important questions about personal responsibility.

Behavioural psychologists such as Skinner used puzzle boxes to systematically investigate learning in animals like rats.

This very strict view of behaviour was introduced by John B. Watson in 1924 and is known as 'methodological behaviourism'. In the 1930s, B.F. Skinner introduced 'radical behaviourism', which proposes that emotion can play a role in our behaviour despite not being directly observable and available for analysis. Skinner also proposed that we do not simply react to a stimulus, but certain factors known as 'operants' affect our reaction and influence the likelihood that a behaviour may be repeated. Operants may be rewards that we experience for a behaviour, or punishments.

CRITICISM

A criticism of many approaches in psychology is that they are 'reductionist', meaning that they reduce the very complex phenomena of human behaviour down to one set of rules or theories, ignoring other factors. This is a necessary process, especially in a branch of psychology such as behaviourism, which seeks to study behaviour in a scientific and empirical way. In order to measure the effect of a variable on behaviour, and in order to investigate its validity as an explanation through repeated testing, we must focus only on that variable. Skinner's radical behaviourism to some extent sought to redress this imbalance.

Despite its limitations, behavioural psychology has contributed to our understanding of learning through experience, of how phobias may be learned in childhood, and even how phobias can subsequently be cured in adulthood. Its processes are used daily in schools to encourage positive behaviour in children, in workplaces to encourage productivity, and even on social media, where it is deployed to keep us clicking the 'like' button.

11
Classical Conditioning

Classical conditioning is a key behaviourist theory that was developed not by a psychologist, but by a Russian physiologist, Ivan Pavlov (1849–1936). Classical conditioning is essentially learning through association – one of the simplest but most effective forms of learning.

PAVLOV'S DOGS

Pavlov was studying the digestive system and in one of his experiments (for which he won a Nobel prize) he was studying salivation in dogs. As part of Pavlov's procedures the dogs were presented with food and their saliva was then collected in a small vial that was surgically attached to their saliva glands. Salivation is a reflex action, meaning that it is something the dogs cannot control. Pavlov wanted to see whether the response could be controlled. In fact, what he found was that the dogs did not only salivate when they were presented with food. They salivated whenever they saw or heard stimuli that reminded them of the arrival of food, such as seeing the assistants who fed them, or hearing their arrival. The dogs had learned to associate the laboratory assistants with a stimulus: food. Anyone with a pet will have experienced similar reactions from their furry friends, for example excited barking when you open the cupboard where the leads are kept. However, Pavlov conducted the first controlled study to examine this phenomenon.

Pavlov began by having his assistants present the dogs with food (the uncon-ditioned stimulus), and at the same time began a metronome clicking (the neutral stimulus). The dogs would salivate in

Pavlov collected saliva by implanting a cannula into the dog's salivary glands.

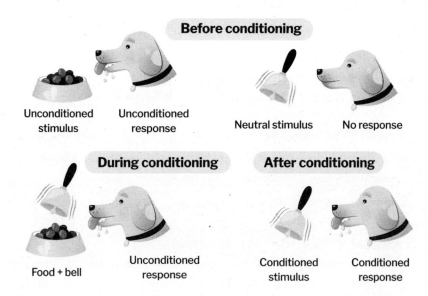

Before conditioning

Unconditioned stimulus   Unconditioned response   Neutral stimulus   No response

During conditioning   **After conditioning**

Food + bell   Unconditioned response   Conditioned stimulus   Conditioned response

Pavlov taught dogs to salivate when they heard a sound they had been conditioned to associate with food.

response to the food (the unconditioned response). This process was repeated until Pavlov felt that the dogs had begun to associate the sound of the metronome (now a conditioned stimulus) with the presence of food. Next, Pavlov and his assistants presented the dogs with only the metronome (the conditioned stimulus) and observed that they began to salivate (the conditioned response) even without the presence of food. The dogs had been conditioned to associate the metronome with food.

Unconditioned stimulus:

A stimulus that naturally produces a reflexive response.

Unconditioned response:

A reflex action or natural behaviour.

Neutral stimulus:

A stimulus that the animal or person does not (yet) associate with the unconditioned stimulus being used.

Conditioned stimulus:

Once the unconditioned stimulus has been associated with the neutral stimulus by repeated exposures, the neutral stimulus becomes the conditioned stimulus.

Conditioned response:

The unconditioned response becomes a conditioned response once it is elicited by the conditioned stimulus alone.

CLASSICAL CONDITIONING IN HUMANS

Conditioning isn't restricted only to animals. It has been used to explain why we might avoid certain foods if they have made us feel ill in the past, why we might feel the urge to eat when adverts come on television, and why we might develop phobias.

One famous and controversial study by psychologists John B. Watson and Rosalie Rayner (1898–1935) attempted to demonstrate the application of classical conditioning in humans by conditioning a phobic reaction in an infant known as 'Albert B'.

Conditioned emotional reactions (Watson and Rayner, 1920)

Watson and Rayner aimed to condition a fear response in a young child using classical conditioning. As unethical as this sounds, Watson and Rayner had intended to reverse the conditioning once the study was finished and didn't mean there to be any long-term psychological damage to the child.

They recruited the child of a nurse at the hospital where they were based, referring to him as 'Albert B'. Through each stage, Watson and Rayner controlled and documented their procedures, even filming some of them.

The procedures took place in the following stages:

Emotional tests:

At nine months old, Albert was presented with various objects to observe his response and check that he was emotionally stable around new objects. Among other things, Watson and Rayner showed him animals such as a white rat, a rabbit, a dog and a monkey.

Session 1: Establishing the conditioned emotional response

At 11 months and three days old they began conditioning Albert to be fearful of a white rat by presenting him with the rat, then banging a metal bar loudly behind him whenever he reached to touch the rat. They called this process 'joint stimulation' and repeated it twice, hoping that Albert would then be conditioned to associate the rat with the unpleasant sound.

Session 2: Testing the conditioned emotional response

A week after conditioning Albert to be fearful of the rat, he was shown the white rat with no scary sound, and given wooden blocks to play with. He reached out carefully to touch the rat, then pulled his hand away, suggesting that he had become fearful of touching it. He played happily with the wooden blocks, showing that he wasn't simply fearful of things that were given to him by Watson and Rayner.

Session 3: Generalization

At 11 months and 15 days old, Watson and Rayner tested whether or not Albert generalized his fear of the white rat on to other fluffy animals and objects. He showed a fear response when they presented him with the rat and a rabbit, a less violent fear response to a dog and a fur coat, and no fear response to cotton wool or Watson's hair.

Session 4: Changing the environment

At 11 months and 20 days old, Albert's fear conditioning was freshened up with a few more joint stimulations using the rat and the loud noise. He was taken to a new space in order to see if his fear response only occurred in the room in which he had been conditioned (a well-lit 'dark room' that was used to develop X-rays at the hospital) or whether he would have the same response elsewhere. He was taken to a large, bright lecture theatre and shown the animals and objects from Session 3 again. His responses to the rat, rabbit and dog were less extreme in this new environment, but still apparent.

Session 5: The effect of time

Finally, Watson and Rayner wanted to see if the fear conditioning wore off over time. They waited until Albert was 12 months and 21 days old before testing him again. They found his reaction to furry objects was less extreme, but still present.

This study showed that children could learn fear through conditioning, and gave fascinating insights into how phobias may develop in early childhood. The gains to psychology may not be outweighed by the costs to Albert B. Watson and Rayner did not get the chance to reverse their conditioning as promised. His mother left the hospital, taking Albert with her, not long after the final session was completed, and whether or not Albert's experiences as a participant in this study had a longer-term effect is unknown.

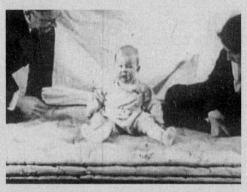

Watson and Rayner working with 'Albert B'. to investigate conditioning in infants.

SYSTEMATIC DESENSITIZATION

Classical conditioning might explain how a human could learn to associate a certain stimulus, such as a spider, with a response, such as fear. Maybe as a child a spider unexpectedly appeared on a person's shoulder, or a family member saw a spider and screamed, startling them. These could have been the first steps towards a person developing a conditioned phobia of spiders. One attempt to apply our knowledge of conditioning usefully has been to reverse this fear conditioning using a process called 'systematic desensitization'.

Systematic desensitization aims to extinguish an undesirable behaviour (fear) by replacing it with a more desirable one (relaxation). The process works by presenting a person with a phobia, such as a fear of spiders, with progressively more fear-inducing scenarios. For example, they may begin by just looking at a drawing of a spider, then a photo, then being in the same room as a toy spider, then touching the toy spider, and so on, finally building up to holding a live spider.

At each step, they are taught to relax using techniques such as controlled breathing or progressive muscular relaxation. The idea is that a person cannot feel two conflicting emotions at the same time, so if they learn to associate feelings of relaxation with seeing a spider, they cannot simultaneously feel fearful. This is known as 'reciprocal inhibition'.

At the end of a desensitization course for arachnophobia, a participant may be encouraged to hold a live spider.

12

Operant Conditioning

Towards the end of the 1930s, B.F. Skinner proposed a new theory of learning: operant conditioning. Skinner had idolized the famous Ivan Pavlov who had first systematically studied learning through association, and built on Pavlov's work to show that it is not only the associations that we make that alter our behaviour, but also the consequences of our actions.

LEARNING THROUGH CONSEQUENCE

Skinner proposed that we learn through reinforcement and punishment. Behaviour that is rewarded (reinforced) is more likely to be repeated, and behaviour that is punished is less likely to be repeated. However, operant conditioning is more complicated than simply rewarding an animal or person for performing a desirable act. Skinner said that: 'The way positive reinforcement is carried out is more important than the amount', and reinforcement and punishment can take different forms and be applied using different schedules.

Both reinforcements and punishments can be negative or positive according to Skinner. It might sound like a contradiction to say that a person can receive a positive punishment, but in this case positive doesn't mean 'good' or 'nice'. It means that something is added to the situation, such as an object or an action. A negative punishment or reinforcement would be a situation in which something was taken away. So for example, a positive reinforcement may

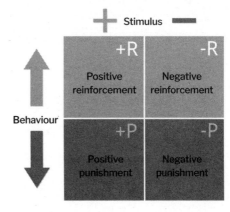

be giving someone a sweet or praise as a reward for behaviour you wish to be repeated. A negative reinforcement may be removing an unpleasant stimulus to reward behaviour, for example your annoying morning alarm noise stopping when you get up and turn it off.

The Behavior of Organisms (B.F. Skinner, 1938)

At Harvard, Skinner developed what he called 'operant conditioning apparatus' to study the effects of reinforcements and punishments on behaviour. His students began calling this apparatus the 'Skinner Box', a name that Skinner himself was not in favour of.

The box contained a lever or a key that an animal could press in order to receive reinforcement, such as a food pellet. A researcher could vary the rate at which the lever or key needed to be manipulated to release a pellet. The box could also contain a stimulus, such as a light, image or sound, which the animal could respond to, and the floor of the box could also be electrified to show how negative reinforcement (the removal of the unpleasant electrocution) might also be used to reinforce behaviour. The results of his studies were published in his 1938 book *The Behavior of Organisms*.

Skinner used these boxes to demonstrate that the rate with which the animal, usually a rat or pigeon, pressed the lever or key was not dependent on preceding stimuli as Pavlov had suggested through classical conditioning, but on what followed the bar presses.

Skinner also used the boxes to investigate the effect of different ratios of reinforcement. If an animal received reinforcement every time they completed an action (continuous reinforcement), they may become habituated to the reward and bored of it, and stop repeating the action. This is known as 'extinction'. Skinner tried varying the reinforcement to see what effect that had:

- *Fixed-ratio schedule*: The animal receives a pellet after they perform an action a certain number of times; for example, a pigeon receiving a pellet after every five pecks of a key.
- *Variable-ratio schedule*: The animal receives reinforcement after a random number of responses.

• *Fixed-interval schedule*: The animal receives reinforcement after a set period of time has elapsed.
• *Variable-interval schedule*: The animal receives a pellet at random intervals of time.

Skinner found that variable ratio schedules, where the reinforcement was unpredictable, were more resistant to extinction.

This knowledge has important applications in our everyday lives. It can be utilized by animal trainers to get desired results by varying the reinforcement that they give to the animal they are training, perhaps by varying when they give rewards or the type of reward. For example, if a dog knows that when they respond to you calling their name you will certainly give them a piece of cheese, they may one day decide that the cheese is less exciting than the squirrel they were planning to chase. If they are unsure of exactly what reward they will receive for returning to you, they may be more willing to gamble on something exciting being provided for them and forget about the squirrel.

This link to gambling can also be applied to humans. Slot machines work on the same principle of variable ratio schedules. Often, the gambler receives nothing, sometimes they receive a small reward, but occasionally they receive a substantial reward, and that uncertainty is what keeps us pulling the lever.

PROJECT PIGEON

During World War II, Project 'Pigeon' (later Project 'Orcon', for 'organic control') was American behaviourist B.F. Skinner's attempt to develop a pigeon-guided missile. Pigeons were placed in front of a screen and taught to peck a target. Each time they pecked the target they received some seed. If the target went off course it would shift to the side of the screen, and by pecking at it the pigeons could return it to the centre and receive their reward. This was intended to keep the missile on target and enable it to deal its devastating blow.

Eventually, the project was abandoned in favour of electronic guiding systems that had become more sophisticated in the meantime.

13

Social Psychology

Social psychology is the study of how our place in society influences our behaviour. It focuses on our social interactions and how they shape us, investigating subjects such as the factors that affect our likelihood to conform to group behaviours, why we obey authority figures, and how small groups and individuals can effect change in society.

The concept of the individual is ingrained in Western society. Unlike collectivist cultures, such as China, which emphasize the importance of the community and the contribution each individual makes to their collective, in individualist societies it is of cultural importance that the individual is recognized as having their own goals and needs, and has autonomy in their actions. It is interesting, then, that the majority of research into social psychology and the loss of individual identity and autonomy has been conducted in these individualist societies.

NORMAN TRIPLETT AND SOCIAL FACILITATION

An 1898 study by psychologist Norman Triplett is widely considered to be the first formal piece of research in the field of social psychology. He noticed that cyclists tended to achieve better times when they were racing against another cyclist rather than attempting to beat a clock. Triplett tested this observation by creating a competitive situation between children (winding in a length of fishing line), and then putting the children in one of two scenarios: 1) completing the task alone; 2) completing the task next to a peer who is performing the same task. Those competing against a peer did indeed perform better.

This is known as the 'co-action effect', and forms part of a larger area of research known as 'social facilitation'. Social facilitation is the idea that an individual will put more effort into a task in the presence of, or even implied presence of, others. You have undoubtedly noticed this effect if you have ever joined a fitness or sports club.

KURT LEWIN AND MODERN SOCIAL PSYCHOLOGY

During World War II, many Gestalt psychologists fled Nazi Germany to the USA. One of these psychologists was Kurt Lewin, who is largely credited with the study of modern social psychology. Lewin coined the term 'group dynamics' to describe how the behaviour of individuals is influenced by their being part of a group.

Psychologists of this era, such as Lewin, had experienced at first hand the profound effects that group behaviour can have on individuals during the rise of the Nazi party in Germany. They had witnessed their countrymen turn on, and even systematically exterminate, people who had previously been their neighbours and friends. So it is unsurprising that social psychologists of the early 20th century would be interested in the study of the effects of groups on individual behaviour. Research

According to social facilitation theory, a lone cyclist is much less likely to achieve their personal best than a cyclist who is competing against others. In this photo, however, British cyclist Mark Cavendish is tackling stage 17 of the Tour de France, a race in which he would actually be competing against many cyclists who are not pictured. Cyclists in Le Tour ride in supportive teams. This tactic has many advantages, one being that cycling with others can help to set the right pace at the right time.

into group dynamics, conformity and obedience all sought to answer questions regarding how our behaviour changes when we are influenced by groups or authority figures.

In the years that followed, social psychology branched in many directions. Research into topics such as the social roles we play, relationships and prosocial behaviour emerged. Researchers investigated how social movements begin, and how even minorities without any obvious authority can influence the behaviour of a larger majority.

CRITICISMS

Research in social psychology can be challenging. If a person is told that they are being observed to see if they will conform to the opinion of a group or obey orders without question, of course they will strive to do the opposite. Studying these concepts under controlled conditions therefore requires deception of participants, and as a result brings into question the ethics of social psychological research.

Well-controlled experiments are often the only way to investigate which factors contribute to a certain behaviour. They have high internal validity, meaning that researchers can be quite sure that the variable they have changed is most likely the one that has resulted in the behaviour they are observing.

However, as with much of psychological research, controlled experiments such as this lack external validity. They may not accurately represent the conditions of real life and therefore how people would behave in real life. Some social behaviours may even be impossible to investigate under controlled conditions, such as the spontaneous incidences of group conformity that might occur during protests or at large festivals. Observing these behaviours in real life is another option, but how is a researcher to predict when a situation will arise that invites conformity or obedience?

Despite these shortcomings, research in social psychology has given us useful insights into how society and our role within it influences our behaviour. It has taught us how to harness our social inclinations to encourage prosocial behaviours, how to motivate ourselves to improve by harnessing the influence of others, but also which factors contribute to social behaviours that can be harmful, such as conforming to a group or obeying others even when we privately feel it is wrong to do so. The findings of this research and the theories that result from it can help us to be better individuals, and better members of our society.

14

Conformity

Humans are social animals. We live in groups and in many ways rely on one another to survive as part of a society that extends beyond us as individuals. We have lived in social groups for many thousands of years, and as a result have developed psychological tendencies that ensure the cohesion of these groups. One of those tendencies is our willingness to conform to the will of a group, even when we know the group may be incorrect or doing something we do not agree with.

Most of us would probably like to think that we do not conform under pressure, and that we are strong-willed and would stand up for what we believe in. However, research evidence shows that this is often not the case.

SOCIAL INFLUENCE

In 1932, Arthur Jenness published his findings from what is considered to be the first research on group conformity, a study titled 'The role of discussion in changing opinion regarding a matter of fact'. He wanted to see if discussion between groups of people, be they small or large, could influence a person's response to a question. He asked individual participants to estimate how many beans were contained in a bottle. He then asked them to join a group, discuss the number of beans, and estimate again as a group, and then finally again individually. He found that very few people could resist the urge to alter their opinion to be closer to that of the group estimate, and that the average change of opinion was greater among women than among men.

Following this early research into conformity came theories to attempt to explain the phenomenon. In 1955, M. Deutsch and H.B. Gerard identified two possible reasons why people conform that are linked to beliefs and motivations:

SOCIAL INFLUENCE THEORY

In 1958, Herbert Kelman introduced his concept of social influence theory. Similar to Deutsch and Gerrard, he proposed that compliance is dependent on our social relationship with the group and what is motivating us to maintain that relationship. He suggested three different types of conformity that depend on these factors:

Normative social influence	Informational social influence
Motivated by a need to gain acceptance from the group.	Motivated by the need to have confidence in their beliefs.
The individual believes that they are being monitored by the group so adjusts their behaviour in order to 'fit in'.	The individual is more likely to accept this type of influence if it is difficult to find information themselves, or the group contains experts.
Privately, the individual may not agree with the beliefs of the group, but they appear to publicly.	Their beliefs change both privately and publicly.
The change in behaviour does not last indefinitely.	The change often lasts for the person's lifetime.

1. **Compliance:** Accepting the will of the group in order to fit in. People accept the influence of a group because they expect to be rewarded if they do, or punished if they do not. Any change in behaviour is usually temporary and stops when group pressure ceases. Compliance is displayed in public but privately held beliefs do not change.

2. **Identification:** Conforming to become a member of the group. People adopt the behaviour or beliefs of a group in order to become part of that group. Any change in behaviour/beliefs is displayed in public but privately held beliefs do not change.

3. **Internalization:** Genuine acceptance of a group belief. People accept the influence of a group because it matches their value system. Their beliefs are genuinely altered to match those of the group. Any change in behaviour/beliefs is displayed publicly, but unlike the other forms of conformity, privately held beliefs also change.

What these theories suggest is that conformity can be the result of us simply wanting to go along with the crowd, maybe for an easy life or to improve our social status, or can be the result of us genuinely identifying with the crowd and having shared beliefs. Whatever our reasons, we are all subject to the effect of social influence at some point in our lives.

Effects of group pressure upon the modification and distortion of judgement (Asch, 1951)

Solomon Asch set out to study the factors that influence conformity. He told participants that they were taking part in an experiment on vision. With a group of other people who were really actors (known as 'confederates'), participants were asked to look at three lines of different lengths and determine which one matched a target line. After a few trials in which everyone stated the correct answer, the confederates all began choosing an incorrect answer. The task was easy enough that the participants should have been confident of their answers, so any incorrect answers that they gave must have been the result of conforming to the belief of the rest of the group. Reassuringly, Asch found that no participants conformed on 100 per cent of the trials they took part in, and 13 out of the original 50 participants did not conform at all. However, 75 per cent of participants conformed and gave an incorrect answer at least once. The highest rate of conformity was a participant who conformed on 11 out of 12 trials. Asch then repeated his study, varying certain factors each time and measuring their effect:

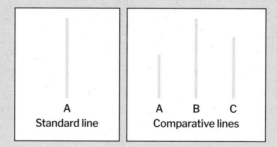

A
Standard line

A   B   C
Comparative lines

Factor	Description and conformity
Size of group	With one confederate present, conformity dropped to 3 per cent; with two, it was at 14 per cent; and with three, conformity peaked at 32 per cent. Further increases in group size did not increase conformity. With very large groups, conformity actually began to fall.
Supporter	If one confederate disagreed with the others and gave the correct answer, conformity dropped by as much as 80 per cent. So, having support makes us less likely to conform.
Difficulty of task	Asch made the comparison lines more similar in length, making the task harder and the correct answer more ambiguous. Conformity increased, which suggests we are more likely to conform when we doubt our own judgement.
Privacy	When participants could answer privately conformity decreased. Presumably with less pressure from the group, participants felt able to stand by their own judgement.

15

Minority Influence

When we conform to the behaviour of a larger group we may be trying to maintain the status quo or not draw attention to ourselves. The urge to fit in is strong, so a majority have to put little effort, if any, into encouraging others to adopt their behaviours. However, conformity can take place without an individual privately changing their opinions or beliefs. When a minority seeks to alter the behaviour of a majority, they must instead work to win over hearts and minds. They have to alter not only a person's public behaviour, but their private beliefs as well. This requires careful communication and co-ordination.

THE BEHAVIOURAL STYLE OF THE MINORITY

When trying to influence a majority, a minority must present their arguments very carefully. Psychologists such as Serge Moscovici argue that there are several key components of behaviour that influence how successful a minority's efforts will be:

- **Consistency:** The minority should present their argument consistently and not deviate. This causes the majority to reassess their own beliefs as the minority appear unwavering in their message.
- **Confidence:** The minority must be confident in their argument, being adamant that their position is the correct one in order to in turn inspire confidence in those who may be won over to their position.
- **Appearing unbiased:** An unbiased argument implies that it is based on reasoning rather than subjective emotional reaction.

Protestors supporting the women's suffrage movement were consistent in their message.

In 1969, Moscovici conducted an investigation into the impact that the consistency of a minority argument has on a majority. In each condition of his study, four participants were placed with two confederates. They were shown images of blue slides that varied in their intensity of colour, and asked to state what colour the slides were. In one condition, the two confederates consistently stated that the slides were in fact green. In another condition, the confederates inconsistently stated for two-thirds of the time that the slides were green, and that they were blue the rest of the time. In the control condition, there were no confederates and participants correctly stated that the slides were blue. What Moscovici found was that the inconsistent minority had very little influence on the majority, but with the consistent minority the majority was influenced to call the blue slides green 8 per cent of the time.

EFFECTING SOCIAL CHANGE

For a minority to bring about social change, there are several stages that they must go through that have been recognized by researchers such as Moscovici. First, the minority must draw attention to the issue at hand and create what is known as a 'cognitive conflict' between what the majority currently believes and what the minority wants them to believe. This can be done through protests and campaigns that clearly highlight

Minorities can prove their commitment to their cause by taking risks in an attempt to raise awareness. Here, two protestors for the group Fathers 4 Justice occupy the exterior of the first floor outside Downing Street.

the current position in society and what the minority wish to achieve.

The minority must then be consistent in their stance to demonstrate their confidence that their point of view is the correct one. For example, the suffragette movement drew attention to their issues through petitions, protests and advertising, which began in the early 1800s and did not end until all women over the age of 21 were granted the opportunity to vote on 2 July 1928. They were consistent in their message over all these years.

In order to prove their commitment to their cause, some minority groups may even put themselves in harm's way or subject themselves to great suffering in order to raise awareness. This is known as the 'augmentation principle'. Some of the best-known examples include Gandhi's use of hunger strikes as a form of passive resistance, suffragettes risking imprisonment to gain votes for women and, more recently, groups such as Fathers 4 Justice dressing in costume and scaling tall buildings to raise awareness of the rights of fathers.

However, a barrier for all minority groups is that humans tend not to want to be seen as different. We inherently wish to be accepted, and if a minority's message deviates too far from the status quo, it risks being labelled as deviant. This risk is increased if we engage in behaviours that are illegal or an inconvenience to others. For example, the criticism received by environmental campaign group Greenpeace sometimes distracts from the message they are attempting to convey. One prime example would be their protest against Volkswagen as a sponsor of the Euro 2020 football tournament, in which a protestor lost control of their motor-powered paraglider and injured two people as they attempted to disrupt play at the football arena in Munich.

16

Obedience

In the wake of World War II, there was much speculation regarding why and how the atrocities of the concentration camps could have occurred. Following the trial of Adolf Eichmann, questions arose surrounding the concept of German soldiers and officials 'just following orders'. Eichmann had been key in planning the strategic identification and transport of condemned people into the concentration camps, but during his trial he'd claimed: 'I couldn't help myself; I had orders, but I had nothing to do with that business.'

Adolf Eichmann was executed in 1962 for his role in enabling the efficiency of the concentration camps, but his insistence that he was just following orders shook people. Eichmann had been examined by six psychiatrists and had been found to be sane and 'normal', so how could he have acted so coldly? In order to address this speculation, a psychologist called Stanley Milgram (1933–84) set out to test how far ordinary people really would go when following orders issued by an authority figure, and what he found shocked the public.

OBEDIENCE TO AUTHORITY

Obedience is a form of social influence that differs from conformity in that an individual acts in response to a direct order from another individual. It is assumed that the person would not have acted in this way without such an order. It involves a hierarchy of power or status, whereby an authority figure directs a person who is subordinate to them. Conformity, on the other hand, is the result of social pressure from a group.

Milgram found that the majority of participants in his study would obey the instructions of an authority figure (a researcher wearing a white lab coat) and electrocute another person whom they could not see, to the extent that the person complained, screamed and then became totally silent. It simply took the presence of an official setting, an official-looking person and the victim being in another room for an average person to commit an act they probably would otherwise never be capable of doing.

Milgram conducted variations on his study and found that if the authority figure was removed, the setting was less prestigious or the participant had to be in the same room as their victim, obedience was reduced. Milgram had thus demonstrated not only that people will follow orders that they feel are immoral, but also the distinct factors that influence how likely a person is to respond to those orders.

In 1981, Bibb Latané (born 1937) set out rules that he believed could explain the findings of researchers such as Milgram. He developed a theory to explain why people conform in some situations but not others.

Behavioural study of obedience (Milgram, 1963)

In a laboratory at Yale University in 1963, Stanley Milgram conducted what was to become an infamous study of obedience to authority. He placed an advert in a local paper and recruited 40 male participants aged 20 to 50.

- The participants were told that they were taking part in a study on learning. They were introduced to 'Mr Wallace', (in fact a stooge working with Milgram). Mr Wallace and the participant drew lots to see who would be teacher and learner, but this was set up so that Mr Wallace was the 'learner'.
- Mr Wallace went into a different room and the participant was shown the equipment. They were told that Mr Wallace would be asked a series of questions and if he answered incorrectly they should give him an electric shock. The teacher was given a 45 volt shock to show that the equipment was real, although it was not and this was the only shock it would give. The participant was told that each incorrect answer from Mr Wallace would result in him receiving a shock 15 volts higher than the last. The researcher encouraged the teacher to administer the shocks with predetermined prompts, such as 'please continue' and 'I am responsible for what happens'.

During the observation, Mr Wallace made various pre-planned noises, such as grunts of pain. At higher voltages, he made statements such as 'Experimenter get me out of here', at 315 volts he let out a violent scream, then from 330 volts onwards he was silent. The observation was considered over when 450 volts was reached or the participant withdrew from the study.

While the study sounds distressing to the participant, all were debriefed following the procedures and met the learner again to see he was fit and well.

Milgram found that all of the participants continued to 300 volts, but five (12.5 per cent) refused to continue after this level; 65 per cent of participants continued to the highest level of 450 volts.

Milgram also recorded qualitative observations of the participants' behaviour. The majority of the participants were convinced that the situation was real and that Mr Wallace was receiving shocks. Many participants showed signs of nervousness and tension. They sweated, trembled, stuttered, bit their lips, groaned and dug their fingernails into their flesh. Three participants suffered seizures, and one participant had a violent convulsive seizure and the experiment had to be stopped.

Milgram concluded that several factors contributed to the high levels of obedience:

1. The prestigious location (Yale University).
2. The researcher wearing a white coat (symbol of a professional).
3. The learner being in a separate room (acts as a buffer).
4. The researcher being physically present and using verbal prods.

FACTORS INFLUENCING OBEDIENCE

First, he proposed that it is dependent on the social force. This is the strength that you believe the person giving you the order has, how immediate the order is (for example, are you being asked face to face or is it an order that has been sent some time ago), and the number of people submitting the order.

Second, he suggested the concept of psychosocial law. This is the idea that increasing the number of authority figures doesn't increase the impact of the order by that same amount. For example, being asked to do something by one authority figure might be quite awkward if you do not obey them, but if you add additional authority figures to the situation it doesn't become more awkward by the same degree. Sometimes fewer authority figures can be more effective.

Finally, he posited that there are divisions of impact. Also known as 'diffusion of responsibility', if many people are being given the order it reduces the impact of the order. Each person will feel less social responsibility to follow the order. Milgram did in fact find that obedience levels fell when the participant had a partner with them who did not obey.

17

Social Roles

As participants in human society, we all take on social roles in one form or another. Teacher, parent, creative – we identify with the expectations of those roles and subconsciously adopt them as our own. In 1973, Philip Zimbardo (born 1933) conducted the infamous Stanford prison experiment to demonstrate this effect. The study was cut short and has many flaws in its methodology, but it still stands as a fascinating example of how the social roles we play in society influence our behaviour.

THE STANFORD PRISON INVESTIGATION

As part of a larger project being run by the Office of Naval Research at Stanford University, Zimbardo and his colleagues sought to investigate the psychological mechanisms that underlie aggression in what they called 'total institution' environments, such as prisons. They replicated conditions in a prison and recruited 22 white male participants, all college students who were strangers to one another. Each was randomly assigned the role of prisoner or guard, and the relationship between the two roles was clearly defined by several measures, for example guard or prisoner uniforms being worn, depersonalization of the prisoners by assigning them numbers, and so on.

What Zimbardo and his colleagues found was that very quickly each participant took on the characteristics that they believed matched their role. Prisoners became submissive and docile, while the guards became aggressive. The extreme psychological reactions of the participants meant that the study, which was meant to have been conducted over two weeks, had to be stopped after only six days.

CRITICISM OF THE STANFORD PRISON INVESTIGATION

One criticism of Zimbardo's study is that the participants were fully aware of being involved in the study and may well have been acting to meet the expectations of the researchers. However, in interviews after the study had finished, both prisoners and guards stated that they were surprised by the way that they had behaved.

Despite the shortcomings of the methodology, Zimbardo's study encouraged further discussion and awareness of the effect that social roles have on our behaviour, and that people may conform to the stereotypes associated with certain social roles. Whether or not prison guards and prisoners in reality act the way that the participants did in this study, the fact is that the participants *believed* that this was how people in those roles behaved, and they lived up to that expectation.

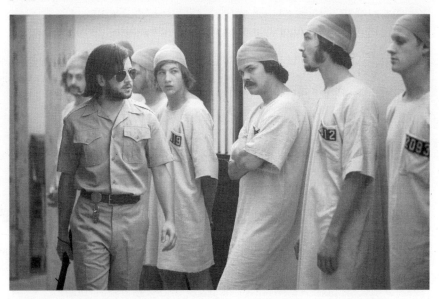

A still from the 2015 docudrama about Zimbardo's study, The Stanford Prison Experiment *showing a 'guard' and 'prisoners'. The name is a misnomer as the study is not a traditional experiment, but rather a controlled observation.*

DEINDIVIDUATION

One explanation given for this behaviour is the concept of deindividuation. This was first introduced in 1895 by Gustave Le Bon (1841–1931) and is discussed in its own chapter later on, but is applied by Zimbardo to explain his observations. The loss of individual identity and personal responsibility on the part of the guards meant that they acted in a way that they may not have done normally.

Zimbardo also suggested the influence of 'learned helplessness' in these situations, specifically in reference to the prisoners and their apparent submission to authority. Learned helplessness occurs when a person is repeatedly exposed to a stressful or traumatic experience and feels that they have no ability to stop it from happening, so they begin to accept it as their reality.

A study of prisoners and guards in a simulated prison (Zimbardo et al., 1973)

Zimbardo and his colleagues recruited 22 white male college students using a newspaper advert. All were strangers to one another. The participants were randomly assigned to one of two roles: prisoner or guard.

The 'prisoners' were informed that they would lose their right to privacy, but would be given basic rights such as adequate food. They were expected to wear loose-fitting smocks, no underwear, a lock and chain around one ankle, and stocking caps to cover their hair. They were also given ID numbers.

The 'guards' wore khaki shirts and trousers and reflective sunglasses, and carried batons. They worked in eight-hour shifts and were allowed to leave the experimental prison when their shift ended.

On a Sunday, police cars arrived at the homes of the 'prisoners' and the subjects were arrested. They were fingerprinted and blindfolded to replicate the emotion of becoming a prisoner, as well as being searched, stripped naked and deloused at the experimental prison. Prisoners were expected to remain in the prison for the duration of the study, and followed a strict schedule of work assignments, rest, toilet and food breaks.

The experiment was planned to take place over two weeks, but had to be stopped after six days. Zimbardo and his team summarized their observations of the effect that the prison environment had on each group:

Prisoners – pathological prisoner syndrome:

* Disbelief followed by rebellion.
* A range of negative emotions and behaviours were reported, including flattened mood.
* Passivity, with some prisoners being very obedient.
* Dependency on guards, for example initiating very little activity without direct instructions.
* Half the prisoners showed signs of depression, crying, fits of rage and acute anxiety and had to be released early.
* Relief when study ended early.

Guards – pathology of power:

* Many seemed to enjoy the power and control that they experienced.
* Began to redefine prisoners' rights as privileges, such as toilet access.
* Punished and verbally insulted the prisoners with little or no justification.
* Some guards volunteered to work extra shifts for no additional pay.
* Continued to behave in an authoritarian way even when they believed that they were not being observed.
* Disappointed when study ended early.

18

Groupthink

Philosopher Friedrich Nietzsche said that madness is the exception in individuals but the rule in groups. While an individual may make rational decisions, when they become part of a group this ability is hampered by additional social pressures. They might feel they must censor legitimate opinions that could be controversial to the group, or have to defer to other group members due to hierarchy. While groups can benefit from shared knowledge, experience and collaboration, they can also fall foul of the phenomena of groupthink, which can lead to irrational decision-making and even disaster.

IRVING L. JANIS

The term 'groupthink' was first used by Irving L. Janis (1918–90) in the 1970s. He described groupthink as a mode of thinking that occurs when people are involved in a highly cohesive in-group, and their need for unanimity and to 'fit in' overrides their own ability to rationally and realistically appraise a situation.

Gestalt psychologist Kurt Lewin also studied group decisions and dilemmas throughout the 1940s, investigating group cohesiveness and conformity. He found that high conformity was more likely when a group experienced high external stress, such as the threat of being injured or killed in combat (or during a space shuttle launch, as we will discuss).

Janis suggested eight symptoms of groupthink:

1. Illusions of invulnerability:
   A group is overly confident and optimistic about their success. This can result in them taking risks that the individual members would not otherwise take.

2. Collective rationalization: Rational reasons are given for decisions being made, or for why others may disagree with certain decisions. In this way, arguments against the collective opinion of the group can be explained away.
3. Belief in inherent morality of the group: The group believes that their moral stance is the correct one, causing them to ignore any moral objections to their decisions.
4. Out-group stereotypes: Out-groups, which are other groups of people who disagree with the group, are stereotyped in ways that make it possible to ignore their opinions. Maybe they are thought of as being ill-informed or lazy. This makes it easier to ignore objections for other groups.
5. Direct pressure on dissenters: If an individual questions a group decision, they are made to feel treacherous and reminded that they can leave the group if they wish.
6. Self-censorship: Group members choose not to speak out against group decisions due to a fear of being ostracized, or a belief that the group knows best.
7. Illusions of unanimity: Lack of disagreement is seen as evidence of good decision-making.
8. Self-appointed mind guards: Members of the group work to actively suppress information or ideas that are contrary to group decisions. They act as censors.

There are thought to be several factors about the nature of a group that make it more susceptible to the pitfalls of groupthink. For example, when members of the group have a strong identity, when they have a charismatic leader, when members of the group either have low knowledge about the task at hand or at least believe that other members have more expert knowledge than them, and when the group is under a large amount of stress.

THE *CHALLENGER* DISASTER: AN EXAMPLE OF GROUPTHINK
One famous situation when many of the contributing factors of groupthink came into play was on the morning of 28 January 1986. On this morning, Christa McAuliffe boarded the Space Shuttle *Challenger*.

The 36-year-old mother of two had been selected out of 11,000 applicants to become the first civilian that National Aeronautical Space Administration (NASA) would launch into space. Her enthusiasm and passion made her the perfect candidate for NASA's 'Teacher in Space' programme. This had reignited interest from the American public in the space programme, with millions watching her train to become an astronaut and hear her speak passionately about space and education.

This was to be the tenth launch of *Challenger* and was intended to showcase that space flight was now routine. NASA hoped that it would revive the ailing Space Shuttle programme, which had been dogged with high costs and political meddling from its outset. For NASA, there was a huge amount riding on this being a successful launch.

The world's eyes were on the shuttle as it blasted off from Kennedy Space Center in Florida at 11.38 am. Seventy-three seconds later, millions of adults and schoolchildren watched on television as the shuttle exploded and disintegrated mid-flight. As the spacecraft plunged into the Atlantic Ocean, a horrified American public knew that all seven astronauts had been killed.

For many, this was viewed as a terrible tragedy but an inevitable risk of space flight. In the following months it became clear that the accident could have, and should have, been avoided.

President Reagan appointed a select committee to investigate the causes of the crash. More than four months of testimonies and evidence-gathering found that a failure of a seal in the joint between two sections of

Christa McAuliffe and her back-up, Barbara Morgan, who were both part of the Teacher in Space project. Morgan successfully flew on the Space Shuttle Endeavour *(STS-118) in August 2007.*

The Space Shuttle Challenger *explodes off the coast of Cape Canaveral, USA, in what is now known to have been a preventable tragedy.*

the rocket booster had allowed hot gas to escape, causing the rocket to explode. It found that NASA had known about the problem prior to lift-off but that a flawed approach to decision-making had allowed the launch to go ahead.

Social psychologist Irving Janis was fascinated by how a group of such highly qualified experts could make such a terrible decision. He was convinced that their poor decision-making was not isolated to the space programme, and believed he could spot the same pattern of flawed decision-making in other tragedies.

He was particularly interested in the decision-making of the White House. In his classic 1972 study 'Victims of Groupthink: A Psychological Study of Foreign-Policy Decisions and Fiascoes', Janis focused on whether the group dynamic he was looking at was present in some of the country's recent political and military disasters, such as Roosevelt's complacency before the Pearl Harbor attack, Truman's invasion of North Korea, Kennedy's Bay of Pigs fiasco, Nixon's Watergate scandal and Reagan's Iran–Contra scandal cover-ups. Janis didn't view the presidents, their advisors or the chief executives at NASA as stupid, lazy or evil. Rather, he saw them as victims of groupthink.

There are several facets of groupthink theory that can be applied to the *Challenger* disaster:

- **Strong sense of group identity**: The *Challenger* team had worked on many missions together.
- **The belief in expert knowledge**: While NASA engineers recommended the launch be postponed, they were isolated from the core decision-making group. A belief in the group's expert knowledge may have caused members of the team not to argue further.
- **The influence of stress**: The launch of the Space Shuttle *Challenger* had already been delayed due to poor weather. With the world waiting

for Christa McAuliffe's historic flight into space, pressure came from politicians and the world's media to launch *Challenger*.

- **Illusions of invulnerability**: NASA had never experienced an in-flight fatality and was riding high in confidence after the rescue in 1970 of the *Apollo 13* crew. When engineers pointed out the shuttle's defective component, the attitude was that this was true for every mission that NASA had flown. Despite defective parts on other rockets these missions had suceeded.
- **Belief in inherent morality of the group**: The space race of the 1960s had put NASA at the forefront of America's moral quest into space to defeat communism. Under the influence of groupthink, engineers at NASA continued with this moral purpose and shifted the rules to suit the overall goal.

For many Americans, the *Challenger* disaster marked the end of their love affair with space. The nation was shocked by the deaths of all seven astronauts, but particularly so by the death of Christa McAuliffe, whom they had come to know closely over the months leading up to the launch. Knowledge of the effects of groupthink can not only explain why a preventable tragedy such as this can occur, but it can also help us to plan strategies to avoid it happening again.

19

The Bystander Effect

Would you walk on by if you saw another person in need of help? Most of us would like to think that we would not, but research suggests otherwise. Living in communities means that we sometimes have a tendency to defer responsibility to those around us. We act as silent observers, not acting when we see an obvious need for help. This behaviour is known as the 'bystander effect'.

THE CASE OF KITTY GENOVESE

The infamous case of Kitty Genovese sparked research into the effect. Kitty was brutally stabbed outside of her apartment in the early hours of a March morning in 1964. After her screams were heard by a neighbour, who shouted for the attacker to 'let that girl alone', the attacker fled and Kitty was able to crawl to the back of her apartment building. Her attacker returned, attacked her again, robbed her and left her for dead. She died on the way to the hospital after being found by a neighbour.

The *New York Times* sparked an outcry when they published an article about the murder titled '37 Who Saw Murder Didn't Call The Police', claiming that many people knew that Kitty was being attacked but did nothing to help her. This claim has since been debunked and it is now believed that in fact only two neighbours knew that Kitty was being attacked and did not act to help her, with one saying 'I didn't want to get involved'.

Kitty Genovese, whose murder led to research into the 'bystander effect'.

Despite this criticism of the sensationalist media coverage at the time, it is still shocking to many of us that anyone could have known that a neighbour was being attacked and not have helped them. We do not believe that we would ever act in such a way. However, this phenomenon has been demonstrated time and time again, and psychologists have long worked to explain the reasons why any of us may be capable of this behaviour.

Good samaritanism: an underground phenomenon? (Piliavin, Rodin & Piliavin, 1969)

Piliavin et al. aimed to investigate whether the apparent reason for a person needing help influenced whether or not bystanders intervened.

They ensured that their research was as realistic as possible by conducting it on public New York subway trains. In total, 4,450 men and women who travelled on a certain train line on weekday lunchtimes were observed. They picked two trains in particular because there were segments of the journey where the train did not stop for seven-and-a-half minutes, allowing plenty of time for the researchers' procedures to take place.

During the procedures, four researchers boarded the train using different doors. Three observed while a male researcher played the victim in need of help.

The victim stood in the centre of the train carriage and as the train passed the first station, they lurched forwards and collapsed. The victim took on one of two personas:

1. The 'drunk' condition – smelling of alcohol and carrying a bottle wrapped in a brown bag.
2. The 'cane' condition – appearing sober and carrying a walking cane.

What the researchers found was that in this real-life scenario, helping behaviour was relatively high; however, it was influenced by the bystanders' perception of the victim's reason for needing help.

The victim in the cane condition received help on 62 out of the 65 trials, whereas the victim in the drunk condition received help on 19 out of 38 trials. Interestingly, during 60 per cent of all of the trials when bystanders offered help, more than one person came forward.

BYSTANDER APATHY

In 1970, psychologists Bibb Latané (born 1937) and John Darley (1938–2018) proposed a decision model to explain the phenomenon of bystander apathy. They stated that individuals tend to feel less responsibility when others are around. Our responsibility is shared, and we feel as though someone else will or should help instead. This is known as 'diffusion of responsibility'. We also suffer from a mindset the psychologists called 'evaluation apprehension'. This is a fear of being judged by others, maybe because our evaluation of the problem is wrong. Finally, we employ 'pluralistic ignorance'. If we should be helping, then why is nobody else helping? Maybe help is not needed or wanted at all.

This model followed a piece of research conducted by Latané and Darley in 1968. In this study, male students were placed in a room on their own. They expected to take part in a discussion via microphone with other students who were also in separate rooms, although in fact the other students' voices were just audio recordings. The discussion was about learning in high-stress environments. During the discussion, one of the pretend students had an audible 'seizure', and Latané and Darley timed how long it took the real student to seek help. They found that the larger the artificial group, the longer it took for the real student to seek help. This suggested that bystander group size is an important influence on how likely we are to provide assistance to someone in need.

In another study, they also found that the reaction of other group members plays a role. When student participants found themselves in a smoke-filled room they were less likely to report the smoke when there were other people present who were not reacting (10 per cent reported the smoke) than when they were alone (75 per cent reported the smoke). Latané and Darley concluded that seeing other people remain passive led the participants to decide that the smoke was not dangerous.

20
Biological Approach

In Leipzig, Germany in 1834, a German anatomist called Ernst Weber (1795–1878) was conducting experiments on sensation. Weber asked his participants to hold two weights, and then gradually increased the mass of one weight until the participant noticed which was heavier. From these studies, he developed Weber's law, which states that the change in a stimulus (such as weight) until it is just noticeable is a constant ratio of the value of the original stimulus.

English psychologist Edward Titchener (1867–1927) would later claim that these studies were 'the foundation stone of experimental psychology'. They certainly influenced a fellow Leipzig University scholar who went on to be credited as the father of experimental psychology, someone we are familiar with from our first chapter: Wilhelm Wundt. In linking his physiological studies with that of perception, Weber conducted some of the earliest research into the relationship between our biology and our psychology.

Now, modern biological psychology encompasses many different approaches: it is used to describe research and theory into subjects such as the influence of evolution, genetics and brain structure. What all of these theories have in common is that they assume that there is a biological cause for our behaviour.

EVOLUTIONARY PSYCHOLOGY

Evolutionary psychology assumes that our behaviours serve a purpose that suited the conditions of our environment of evolutionary adaptiveness. This does not refer to a specific environment or place, but rather a specific set of circumstances that put evolutionary pressure on a species. For humans, it is widely assumed that we spent the majority of our evolutionary past living in an environment that was quite different to the one in which we find ourselves now. We would have lived in smaller communities spending much of our time hunting and gathering food and resources, and our physical and psychological reactions would have evolved to be adaptive to this way of life.

This approach is useful in explaining our adverse reaction to modern stressors that we cannot use our 'fight-or-flight' reflex to deal with (see Chapter 41), in explaining how our intelligence may have evolved (see Chapter 34), and also the purpose of many of our positive behaviours, such as kindness and altruism. If our behaviours are focused on ensuring the survival of our genes, then ensuring that our closest genetic relatives are safe and cared for makes sense. This might include prioritizing their well-being, but could also be influenced by how successful our community is, and so explains seemingly selfless acts of kindness.

The case of Phineas Gage (1848)

In 1848, Phineas Gage, an American railway construction foreman, survived a horrific accident where a 109 cm (43 in)-long iron rod exploded up through his jaw and out of the top of his head. His frontal lobe was damaged but he survived. However, reports suggest that the injury to his frontal lobe altered his previously calm personality and behaviour, and he became notably short-tempered and moody.

This event preceded a large step forward in our understanding of the link between the brain and behaviour, and how individual structures that make up our brain are linked to specific behaviours, personality traits and functions. This is what is now known as 'localization of function'.

CRITICISM

Some find this deterministic, biological view of human behaviour distressing. Are we only kind because it is evolutionarily advantageous for us to be so? Is everything that makes us who we are really bound up inside of our skull? There is also some argument that a medical model of psychology ignores other factors that may influence behaviour, such as our environment or individual psychological differences.

Yet despite any misgivings, biological approaches in psychology offer us many real-life applications that enhance human well-being. For example, drug therapies have been developed using our knowledge of neurotransmission to treat issues such as depression and anxiety, neurosurgeries have been effective in treating conditions such as epilepsy, and advances in brain scanning techniques have even enabled us to communicate with patients who are completely paralyzed.

21

Localization of Function in the Brain

Around 2,500 years ago, the ancient Greek physician Hippocrates (c.460–370 BCE) first argued that the brain was responsible for thought and consciousness. Prior to this, philosophers believed that the heart ruled the head, and we still refer to being 'led by our hearts' when emotional matters are concerned.

The earliest reference to the brain can be traced to an ancient Egyptian document from the 17th century BCE. 'The Edwin Smith Surgical Papyrus', named after the American antique dealer who purchased it in 1862, describes structures of the brain such as the meninges (see next paragraph) and cerebral fluid, and also documents several forms of brain injury and the complications linked to them, including a fracture to the skull that resulted in a patient being unable to talk. This shows that we have, in fact, known for thousands of years that there is a link between our brain and our behaviour. However, it is only relatively recently that we have been able to study a living brain without killing the patient in the process, and as technology advances we are learning more and more about the link between the physical matter of the brain and the intangible qualities of the mind that make us who we are.

The brain is an organ consisting of many different sections and tissues, from the outermost layers of connective tissue called the meninges that cover and protect the brain, to the innermost clusters of nuclei (clusters of neurons), such as the basal ganglia, which are responsible for things like motor control. But what we most commonly think of as 'the brain' and what will be discussed in more detail here is the big, lumpy, cauliflower-like organ formed from grey and white matter.

GREY MATTER AND WHITE MATTER

The grey matter of the brain is made up of the cell bodies of neurons. We will talk about neurons in more detail in Chapter 23, but essentially the grey matter is where most of the brain's processing takes place.

The white matter of the brain is found underneath the grey matter and towards the centre of the brain and is formed mainly from structures called axons, which are specially adapted to pass electrical signals called impulses from the brain to the spinal cord.

THE STRUCTURE OF THE BRAIN

The brain can be divided into sections from the outside in, and each section is associated with different functions. 'Cortex' means 'bark' in Latin, and much like bark on the outside of a tree, the cerebral cortex of the brain is the outermost layer of tissue. Despite being only a few millimetres thick, it is folded in such a way that it creates a large surface area, and actually makes up around half of the mass of the brain. The cerebral cortex creates connections with other structures that form the inner workings of our brain, and so is where much of our thinking, sensing and voluntary movements are co-ordinated.

The cerebellum is the large, bulbous structure found at the back of the brain. It is associated with our voluntary movement, taking instructions from the brain about what we want to do, and co-ordinating it with information from the spinal cord that indicates our position and balance. This ensures that all of the tiny muscular adjustments that need to take

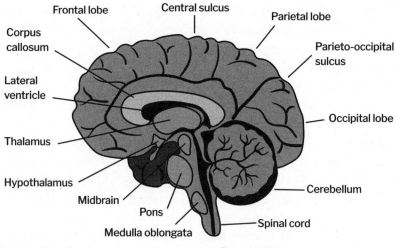

Parts of the brain

place for us to pick up a cup of tea happen without us even being aware of it.

The basal ganglia are found at the base of the brain (hence the name 'basal') and are also involved in movement and co-ordination, and form connections with other areas of the brain, too.

The brainstem is where the brain is connected to the rest of our nervous system via the spinal cord, which joins the brainstem at the medulla oblongata. As well as acting as a connection to the rest of the body, the brainstem has some other key functions. For example, the medulla oblongata plays an important role in regulating essential functions such as our heart rate. A part of the brainstem called the pons houses nuclei that are associated with touch, pain and swallowing, among others.

Finally, the midbrain, the uppermost part of the brainstem, contains nuclei associated with actions such as eye movement, vision and hearing. Degeneration in an area of the midbrain called the substantia nigra, which is actually also part of the basal ganglia, is linked to movement control problems that we see in people suffering from Parkinson's disease, which makes sense when we realize the important role these areas of the brain play in our movement and co-ordination.

THE LOBES OF THE BRAIN

The brain is also divided into two halves – the left hemisphere and the right hemisphere – and each hemisphere is further divided into four lobes, separated by large grooves in the cerebral cortex called sulci. Each lobe is associated with different functions. However, many of these overlap and are hard to define, so the functions are often simplified to give a general overview for each lobe.

The frontal lobe, for example, is associated with cognition, learning, decision-making and planning. It is for this reason that many patients suffering mental illness in the middle of the 20th century were given frontal lobotomies in order to make them more placid. The practice began to be seen as unethical as the century progressed, and by the 1970s, most countries had banned its use.

THE CORPUS CALLOSUM

Each hemisphere is connected by a thick tract of nerves called the corpus callosum, which allows signals to pass from one hemisphere of the brain to the other. The importance of this connection was made very obvious following treatment of people suffering from severe epilepsy

The brain consists of two hemispheres (right and left), each separated into four lobes.

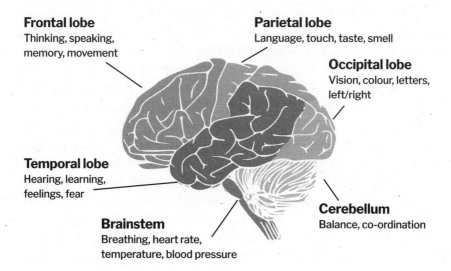

Frontal lobe
Thinking, speaking,
memory, movement

Parietal lobe
Language, touch, taste, smell

Occipital lobe
Vision, colour, letters,
left/right

Temporal lobe
Hearing, learning,
feelings, fear

Cerebellum
Balance, co-ordination

Brainstem
Breathing, heart rate,
temperature, blood pressure

in the 1940s. The treatment involved 'splitting' the brain of the patients by severing the corpus callosum and reducing the chance of epileptic seizure spreading from one side of the brain to the other.

While the procedure did indeed reduce epileptic seizures, there were some unexpected side effects resulting from the two sides of the brain no longer being able to communicate effectively. One patient in particular, known as 'W.J.', took part in a study conducted by a psychologist called Roger W. Sperry (1913–94), during which he was shown stimuli (images of a box or circle) and asked to say what he saw each time. Sperry asked W.J. to fixate on a dot in the middle of a screen, then flashed the images to either W.J.'s left or right field of view.

Sperry knew that each field of view is processed by the hemisphere of the brain on the opposite side, so the right field of view is processed by the left hemisphere of the brain, and vice versa. What Sperry discovered was that W.J. responded normally to stimuli processed by his left hemisphere and was able to verbally state what he saw. With stimuli presented to his right hemisphere, however, W.J. said that he saw nothing. Sperry then asked W.J. to instead simply point every time he saw an image. In this scenario, W.J. could point with his right hand to objects presented to his left hemisphere, and point with his left hand to objects presented to his right hemisphere. This study therefore showed that each hemisphere can process what we see and act on it mechanically by, for example, pointing, but only the left hemisphere can allow us to talk about it.

This is not necessarily as negative as it may sound. There are examples of young patients treated for epilepsy who have undergone full hemispherectomies – complete removal of half of their brain – and while they have lost vision and use of their arm on the opposite side to the removed hemisphere, they have been found to lead otherwise fully functioning lives and even improve academically in the absence of seizures. What the brain teaches us again and again is that localization of function is incredibly complex, and the brain will always surprise us with its ability to adapt.

22

Brain Scanning Techniques

Human investigation of the brain and brain surgery is an ancient art. Evidence of trepanation – creating a hole in the skull to expose the brain – can be found from as long ago as the Stone Age and is claimed to be the earliest form of neurosurgery. The practice is still performed today, although it is now more commonly known as a 'craniotomy' and is only performed after other more sophisticated imaging of the brain has taken place. The technology that allows us to do this represents a huge advance.

For much of human history we could only observe the inner structures of the brain once a person had died, so studying a living brain was impossible. We have since come a long way in our understanding of the brain and how we can study it without, in most cases, needing to perform any surgery at all. In this chapter, we will investigate these brain imaging techniques that allow us to see structure and activity in the brains of living people.

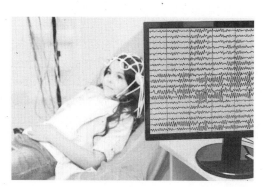

Electroencephalography involves measuring the brain's electrical activity.

ELECTROENCEPHALOGRAPHY (EEG)

One of the most accessible ways to study the activity of the brain due to its ease and relatively low cost, electroencephalography (EEG) allows us to measure the activity of the surface of our brain by recording electrical activity from the scalp and displaying it on a monitor.

Although EEGs do not show us the structure of the brain, they can show us changes in the activity of a person's brain, and so can be used to diagnose conditions such as epilepsy, sleep disorders, brain damage and even tumours.

COMPUTED TOMOGRAPHY SCAN (CT SCAN)

Computed tomography (CT) scans were first introduced in 1971 by Godfrey Hounsfield (1919–2004), an electrical engineer who won a Nobel prize for his role in its development.

CT scans use X-rays and a computer to create detailed images of the inside of the body. The X-rays are delivered in narrow beams by a rotating tube, which can detect hundreds of different levels of density and so build up a detailed three-dimensional picture. Although they cannot show activity in the brain, they can identify damage to bone and tissue and issues with blood flow.

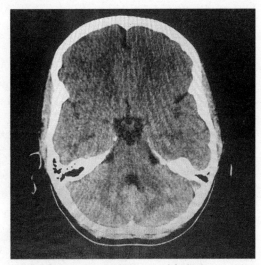

A computed tomography (CT) scan of the brain.

POSITRON EMISSION TOMOGRAPHY (PET)

Used by Adrian Raine (born 1954) in his study of the brains of murderers (see Chapter 46), positron emission tomography (PET) scans can be used to observe activity within the brain. A person drinks, or is injected with, a mildly radioactive substance called a tracer. The tracer pools in areas of the brain that are active and therefore have increased blood flow. As the tracer breaks down, it releases gamma radiation that can be picked up by a receiver. PET scans can be used to detect tumours as tumours will require increased blood flow, which is detected by the scan.

PET scans lack the structural detail of other imaging techniques and cannot pinpoint the activity in the brain at a specific time, rather over a period of time. As a consequence, functional magnetic resonance imaging (fMRI) is increasingly used instead of ET scans when detailed information about brain activity is needed.

MAGNETIC RESONANCE IMAGING (MRI) AND FUNCTIONAL MAGNETIC RESONANCE IMAGING (FMRI)

As the name implies, magnetic resonance imaging (MRI) involves placing a patient inside a large magnet. The strength of the magnet causes the positively charged protons that are found inside the atoms in our bodies to line up with the direction of the magnetic field. When the magnet is switched off, they return to their original positions while releasing electromagnetic waves. These waves are detected by a scanner and an image is produced. The protons in different tissues in the body take different amounts of time to return to their original positions, so different structures in the brain can be seen.

An advantage of MRIs is that unlike CT and PET scans, they do not use a source of radiation to build an image and are therefore considered to be risk-free. However, MRI cannot be used on patients with pacemakers

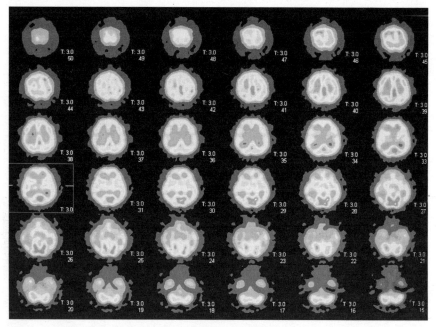

PET scan of a human brain. Red areas show higher activity.

or metal supports within their body. MRIs also only show a snapshot of the brain's structure and not the activity within the brain. This is where functional magnetic resonance imaging (fMRI) comes in.

fMRI scans use blood flow to study brain activity. Oxygen is delivered to cells in the body and the brain by red blood cells, which contain haemoglobin. The magnetic property of haemoglobin is different when it is carrying oxygen compared to when it is not, so once a red blood cell has delivered its oxygen load to a cell its magnetic property changes. When an area of the brain is more active it requires more oxygen, and an fMRI scan can sense this oxygen delivery by detecting the changes in the magnetic property of the haemoglobin.

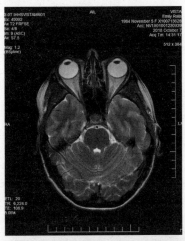

An fMRI scan taken during working memory tasks.

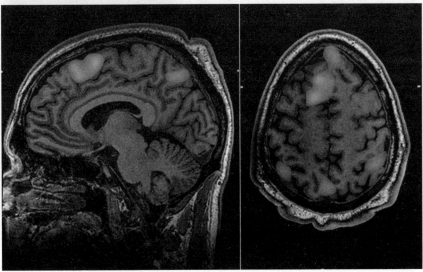

Among other applications, fMRIs have been used to communicate with patients who are in a seemingly vegitative state and would otherwise have no way to communicate with the outside world. The patient can be asked a question, then provide a 'yes' or 'no' answer by activating their brain in certain ways that can be detected. The patients can thus be asked if they are in pain and require medication, whether they want to listen to certain music, or even just confirm that they are conscious. Doctors who work with patients such as this also report that knowing their loved one is conscious and aware of them encourages family members to visit and interact with them more enthusiastically. In this way, the patient's quality of life can be improved immeasurably.

23

Neurotransmission

The brain and spinal cord make up the central nervous system, which is what really makes us who we are. The rest of the body is like a machine working to keep the brain nourished and safe. The central nervous system consists mainly of two types of cells: neurons and glial cells. Glial cells support the neurons, but ineurons are responsible for the electrical information exchange that occurs all over our bodies to enable us to think, co-ordinate and keep the body running.

IMPULSES

The billions of neurons that make up part of our body's communication network pass constant electrical signals, called impulses, to one another at speeds of around 119 m/s (130 yards/s). Even the smallest changes in the environment are detected by receptor cells all over our bodies, such as on our skin or in our eyes, which then convert these changes into electrical signals that are picked up by neurons and carried to glands or muscles, or other effectors in the body that respond to the change in stimulus.

We are not aware of most of the responses our body has to these stimuli – it just quietly processes the information and makes changes to things like our heart rate or pupil dilation so that we can comfortably carry on with our day.

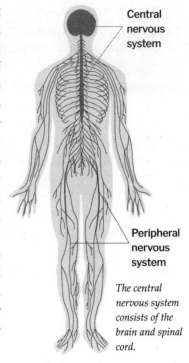

Central nervous system

Peripheral nervous system

The central nervous system consists of the brain and spinal cord.

CONNECTIVITY

In the brain, these impulses travel from one neuron to another, facilitating the cognition that makes us who we are. Attempts have been made to use a special type of MRI to create a 'connectome', a map of these neural pathways in the brain, and better understand these complex connections.

The Human Connectome Project used scans of the brains of around 1,200 people to identify millimetre-wide tracts of nerve fibres that connect different regions of the brain. What they produced is known as a 'macroconnectome', since measurements in millimetres are actually considered quite big when talking about brain anatomy.

Using this technology, scientists from the project have been able to identify fascinating insights, such as the discovery that people who tend to experience low mood or anxiety have fewer connections between the amygdala, a structure in the brain associated with memory, fear and emotional response, and other areas that are related to attention.

Neurons are specially adapted to carry and pass on electrical impulses to one another. They have a long cell body so that they can carry information over relatively long distances, and are covered in a fatty layer called the myelin sheath, which insulates them and allows electrical impulses to travel quickly along the neuron. They also have many branches at either end, called dendrites and axon terminals, which allow each neuron to make many connections with the neurons around it.

Neurons are not physically connected to one another. They use chemical messengers called neurotransmitters to carry the impulse from the axon terminal of one neuron to the dendrite of another across a gap called a synaptic cleft. When an impulse reaches the synapse at the end of the axon terminal, it is picked up by a neurotransmitter which travels across the synaptic cleft, and is picked up by a receptor on a neighbouring dendrite. The impulse is released and can continue its journey around the brain or body.

NEUROTRANSMITTERS

Each neurotransmitter is associated with different behaviours but it is not as simple as associating each hormone with a different emotion. While dopamine, for example, is certainly linked to mood, overactive dopamine pathways in the brain are also associated with certain symptoms of schizophrenia, such as hallucinations, and if your body does not produce enough dopamine it can induce some of the physical symptoms in people suffering from Parkinson's disease, for example tremors.

A 'connectome' is a map of the neural connections in the brain.

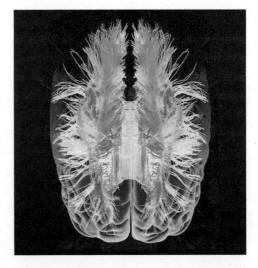

Despite the complexity of neurotransmitters and their relationship to our behaviours, we have developed ways to adjust them in order to treat the symptoms of mental health conditions. For people suffering from depression, drugs called selective serotonin reuptake inhibitors (or SSRIs) can be prescribed to alleviate their symptoms. As the name suggests, SSRIs inhibit the reuptake of serotonin by neurotransmitters. When a neurotransmitter is released at an axon ending, not all of that neurotransmitter reaches the next neuron. Some is reabsorbed by the neuron or broken down by an enzyme. SSRIs such as prozac thus reduce the rate that serotonin is reabsorbed by nerve endings, which increases the amount of serotonin available to neighbouring cells. In people experiencing depression, the increased availability of serotonin can help to relieve their symptoms. Some drugs can also block the enzyme that breaks down neurotransmitters.

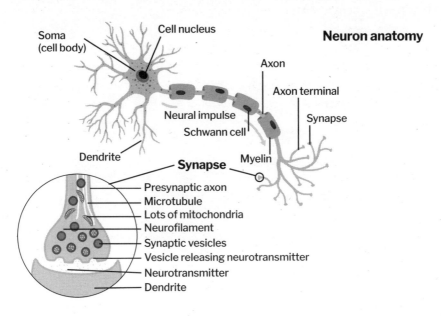

Drug therapies such as this can be very useful as they can work more quickly than talking therapies, and require less effort from the patient. For people who have found that their condition has left them unable to function and make positive changes to improve their health, this can be a first step to improving their situation. However, drug therapies can be addictive, have side effects, and only treat the physical symptoms. They do not alter the underlying psychological, social or environmental causes that may have led to the person becoming unwell in the first place, and they do not stop these issues from continuing to affect the patient in the future.

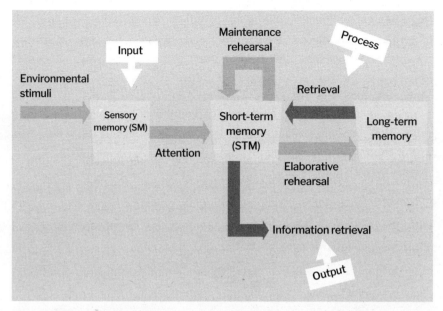

that occur between stimulus and response. By carefully controlling and manipulating conditions in a study, cognitive psychologists can analyze outcomes and *infer* what is happening in the mind.

THE COMPUTER ANALOGY

A key feature of the cognitive approach is that it compares the human mind to a computer. Computers receive input through their interface with the environment, they process that input through coding and memory, and then they produce output by displaying an image or text on a screen, for example. Cognitive psychologists assume that the human mind works in a similar way: we receive input from our surroundings via our senses, process that input through cognitive functions such as attention or memory retrieval, and then produce output in the form of our response. The multi-store model of memory (which is discussed in more detail in the next chapter) is a good example of this assumption being put into action.

The multi-store model of memory is an example of a psychological model that is based on the cognitive assumption of the computer analogy.

INTERNAL MENTAL PROCESSES

The internal mental processes work together to help us to make sense of the world. Four well-known examples are perception, attention, memory and language (see table on page 114):

SCHEMAS

Cognitive psychologists also suggest that experience plays an important role in our processing. They believe that during our lifetimes we gather knowledge and build up packets of information known as 'schemas'. These schemas become more and more detailed over time and help us to categorize, organize and interpret information. For instance, we may develop a schema for what constitutes a certain object (if it has four legs and a flat top it is a table), or a schema for a given situation (sitting quietly when in a cinema). Schemas are very useful for helping us to process the overwhelming amount of new information we encounter each day. However, they can also lead us to make errors if we apply them incorrectly. This may explain why we can be tricked by optical illusions.

Process	Example
Perception	When you see an object or animal such as a dog, you may perceive features that you know are common to dogs, for example four legs, waggy tail, etc.
Attention	You pay attention to features that you think might be important, or that you have seen before.
Memory	You search your memory to find a 'match' for these features.
Language	You use language to label the object: 'dog'.

Reconstruction of automobile destruction: an example of the interaction between language and memory (Loftus and Palmer, 1974)

Investigating how memory works is a much more complicated task for psychologists than the simple testing of memory, and is a good example of how cognitive psychologists manipulate variables in order to be able to infer what may be going on inside the 'black box'.

Our memories are often not an accurate recording of events, but rather an elaborate reconstruction that our mind creates for us. Elizabeth Loftus (born 1944) and John Palmer investigated how language may play a role in the formation of our memories with a study that took place in two halves.

In the first experiment, participants were shown a video of a car accident. Afterwards, they were asked a series of questions about the crash, including one critical question (the one Loftus and Palmer were really interested in) that required them to estimate the speed that the car was travelling at the time of the accident. However, not all participants were asked this question in the same way. They were split into five groups, and each group was asked the critical question using a different verb to describe the accident. One group was asked 'about how fast were the cars going when they smashed each other?', whereas in each of the other groups the verb 'smashed' was swapped for 'collided', 'bumped', 'hit' or 'contacted'.

What Loftus and Palmer found was that the more aggressive the verb, the higher the participants' estimates were. This shows that the language used to question an eyewitness to an event can affect the accuracy of their memory.

Verb used in critical question	Average speed estimate (mph)
Smashed	40.8
Collided	39.3
Bumped	38.1
Hit	34.0
Contacted	31.8

In the second experiment, participants watched a video of a crash and again were asked a series of questions afterwards. This time, the participants were split into three groups. One group was asked what speed the cars were travelling when they 'smashed' into each other, another when they 'hit' into each other, and a third group was not asked about the speed of the cars at all. A week later, participants were asked 'Did you see any broken glass?' Despite no broken glass being evident in the video, a significant number of the 150 participants reported seeing it, most of whom were from the 'smashed' verb group. This experiment demonstrated that post-event questioning can in fact cause witnesses to recall details that did not occur, as well as affecting the accuracy of their memory regarding things that did occur.

Participant response	Verb condition		
	Smashed	Hit	Control
Yes	16	7	6
No	34	43	44

A criticism of this research is that of 'ecological validity'. To have ecological validity it must closely replicate a real-life scenario, so psychologists can be confident that what they saw during their study was an accurate representation of how people would behave in real life. In the case of Loftus and Palmer's research, their experimental conditions deviate from real life in several ways that may well affect the functioning of a person's memory. The participants were watching a video rather than being present at a real car crash. This means that their experience of the crash was very different to a real-life experience – the shock, the sound, the personal feeling of peril, all of which could reasonably affect the workings of a person's memory.

Despite this shortcoming, research such as that conducted by Loftus and Palmer has had an important influence on areas of our lives where accurate and unbiased recall is essential, for example in questioning eyewitnesses to a crime. As a result of our knowledge of the impact of questioning on memory, the cognitive interview was developed, which aims to avoid adding any unnecessary detail to a person's memory or inadvertently altering their recall of the event. An interviewee will be asked to simply describe everything they remember of an event, rather than being asked specific leading questions about facts that may be of interest to the interviewer. In this way, interviewers can be sure that while a witness's memory may still be fallible, they have done what they can to gather honest and complete information.

26

Memory Models

The renowned filmmaker Luis Buñuel (1900–83) wrote: 'A life without memory is no life at all.' Without memory, you could not recognize these letters, the individual meaning of each set of abstract lines that makes a letter or the meaning of their arrangement into words. You would not remember who you are or what you enjoy.

For this reason, illnesses that affect memory can be incredibly distressing for individuals but also their loved ones, who may feel in many ways that with the loss of memory comes the loss of the person. However, amnesia is never as profound as it is portrayed in the movies. Memory is a complex set of processes that include short-term memory, long-term memory, sensory memory and working memory, which all combine to create what we consider to be our memories.

The study of memory often falls to cognitive psychologists, who attempt to study our internal mental processes. Unlike behavioural psychologists, who focus only on observable and measurable behaviours (such as B.F. Skinner, who is discussed in Chapter 12), cognitive psychologists believe that by manipulating the stimuli they give to their participants and then observing the outcome they can infer what may be going on in between, inside the 'black box' of the mind. As a result, there are several models of memory put forward by cognitive psychologists, each of which has its merits in explaining the complexity of memory.

THE MULTI-STORE MODEL OF MEMORY

The multi-store model of memory was first introduced in 1968 by Richard Atkinson (born 1929) and Richard Shiffrin (born 1942). This model proposes that stimuli from the environment first pass through our sensory register, which relates to our physical senses, such as sight or hearing. These stores have a huge capacity so can process a lot of information, but it is only stored here for a very short time before being moved on to short-term memory.

Information passes to our short-term memory store only if we pay attention to it. The short-term memory store has a limited capacity and duration (see Chapter 27 for more information about this), so information can quickly leave it if we do not do something to help it stay there a little longer, or help it move on to our long-term memory store.

Maintenance rehearsal is one way that we can make information stay in our short-term memory a little longer, an example being when you are told a new phone number and you repeat it to yourself over and over again until you are ready to dial it in. However, it is unlikely that you will remember that same number again later in the day unless you have committed it to your long-term memory. The long-term memory store has an infinite capacity and infinite duration, so we can remember experiences or information from even our very early childhood if it has made it to this region.

This model is very useful in helping us to understand why repetition and rehearsal of information makes us more likely to remember it – a particularly useful fact for students. It also helps to explain why we may be able to remember the very last thing a person has said when confronted with an angry 'What did I just say?!' after our minds have wandered midway through a conversation. However, some psychologists argue that this model is too simplistic. The idea of maintenance rehearsal can explain why some information is committed to long-term memory, but not why memories of single episodes in our lives that we have not consciously rehearsed can stay with us forever. Some psychologists also argue that short-term and long-term memory shouldn't be thought of as two single stores, but actually that there can be different types of short- and long-term memory, which can be better explained by the working memory model.

THE WORKING MEMORY MODEL

The working memory model was proposed by Alan Baddeley (born 1934) and Graham Hitch in 1974 and is useful in elucidating some phenomena that cannot be explained by the multi-store model. For example, it can explain why we can perform two tasks at the same time so long as they use two different types of short-term memory store, but if they both require the capacity of the same store we will find them much more difficult

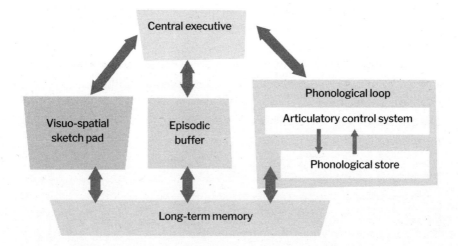

to complete. Thus, we might find it difficult to read while also reciting the words to a song, since both require us to articulate and understand language, but we may be able to recite the words to a song while also completing a jigsaw puzzle, as the puzzle requires us to process visual information but not language.

The working memory model proposes that information we receive is processed by a part of memory called the central executive. The central executive is not really a store, but rather a processor that decides which information we should focus on, then directs it to different memory stores. Visual or spatial information will be passed to the visuo-spatial sketchpad, which also processes visual information that has been stored in our long-term memory, for example if we try to recall the layout of our home. Information relating to language or sound, which includes written information, is passed to the phonological loop. This is further divided into the phonological store, which stores the things we hear or read for a couple of seconds, and the articulatory process, which loops the words that we read or hear so that they remain in our memory. It also processes information that we read and turns it into articulatory code so that it can be passed on to the phonological store.

This model is supported by numerous studies of patients with memory loss. One famous example is the 1974 study by Timothy Shallice (born 1940) and Elizabeth Warrington (born 1931) of a patient known as 'KF', who could remember verbal but not visual information immediately after it was presented to him. This suggests that there may indeed be different short-term processing of the two different types of information. However, there are still questions raised by psychologists regarding the central executive and its role and the over-reliance on studies of brain-damaged patients, who may have other complex reasons for the difficulties they encounter with certain memory tasks.

27

Coding and Short-term Memory

With the development of computers and electronic communication towards the end of World War II, scientists gained a better understanding of how information is communicated. In 1948, Claude Shannon (1916–2001) took his passion for cryptology and code-breaking to investigate further how data is compressed, encoded and transmitted.

These groundbreaking theories created the foundations of 'information theory' whereby information is treated as binary 'bits' and the notion arose that there are limits in the capacity of how much data can be transmitted and then be accurately interpreted at the receiving end of the communication.

Initially, these theories were first used by the Bell Telephone Company for mechanical messaging, but by the end of the 1950s and into the 1960s, information theory began to be applied to human memory. In 1956, George A. Miller (1920–2012) published his famous paper 'Magical Number Seven, Plus or Minus Two: Some Limits on Our Capacity for Processing Information'. He borrowed the vocabulary and concepts from Shannon and information theory to talk about human working memory having channels, information, capacity and coding.

SHORT-TERM MEMORY AND THE MAGIC NUMBER SEVEN

Miller reviewed publications into short-term memory and perception over a 20-year time period, from the 1930s to the 1950s. He noticed similarities in how well people remembered auditory, visual and number sequences. From his research, Miller found that individuals were capable

Claude Shannon with his electrical mouse with a super-memory (1959).

of holding five to nine pieces of information in their short-term memory. He termed this the 'magical number seven plus or minus two'.

One of the first experiments in this area by Joseph Jacobs (1854–1916) in 1887 used a digit span test, essentially recalling a sequence of numbers, to investigate the ability of female students at Collegiate School in North London. The number of digits and letters was gradually increased until the sequence could not be recalled by the participants. Jacobs found that the students had an average recall of 7.3 letters and 9.3 numerical digits. This further supported the notion of Miller's magic number.

Miller explained these results in terms of capacity limits in how the human mind processes information, much like the bandwidth of an internet connection limiting how much information you are able to download into your computer.

Unlike computers, though, humans don't encode data as individual bits of data. Miller noticed that humans use tricks to link data and aid recall by 'chunking' information. Consider how you read a sentence, for example. You have trained yourself to recognize the words (chunks) and have rehearsed the individual letters that make up the words so you have a strategy that allows you to recall more than seven bits (in this case letters) of information. However, Miller did not go on to define exactly what he meant by a 'chunk' of information, and the magic number remained as seven plus or minus two.

For the next 40 years there was little attempt to refine this figure. Miller's interests now lay elsewhere and writing in 1989 he indicated that the article was based on a public address he had been cajoled into giving to the Eastern Psychological Association, and said he was unsure why the paper had gained so much popular interest.

In recent years, the magic number has come back into the spotlight. Its importance in education, communication of public information and marketing are more important now than ever before. Consider the

Covid-19 pandemic. A long public health message with more than nine chunks of information would generally be poorly understood and the key messages not remembered, with potentially disastrous consequences. Short, memorable phrases are much more successful, for example: 'hands, face, space'.

Recent studies by L. Cowen (1926–2000) have attempted to examine the circumstances around how the information is encoded and the effects of time on this process, which Miller did not investigate in his literature review. Miller would go on to say that he thought the figure for the magic number was probably less than seven chunks as he had not included factors such as the effects of time and the age of participants in his study.

Despite the debate around Miller's magic number and the 40 years of stagnation in researching capacity limits in terms of short-term memory, the magic number of seven plus or minus two has remained relatively fixed in psychology. Perhaps it was the entertaining way in which Miller presented his review that gained it such notoriety. Nevertheless, it is one of the most important concepts in the study of short-term memory and is perhaps reassuring since it posits that unlike computers, the human memory cannot simply be programmed with bits of information.

CODING IN SHORT-TERM AND LONG-TERM MEMORY

In 1966, Alan Baddeley investigated whether there were coding differences between short-term and long-term memory. It had already been shown that short-term memory recall for word sequences was much worse when the words sounded similar ('acoustic similarity'), but when they had similar meaning ('semantic similarity') there was little difference. Baddeley wanted to investigate whether the same was true for long-term memory.

Baddeley asked participants to memorize short words from a list of ten. There were four different sets of word lists:

1. Acoustically similar words, (e.g. pan, pad, pap).
2. Acoustically dissimilar words (e.g. hen, day, few).
3. Semantically similar words (e.g. small, tiny, little).
4. Semantically dissimilar words (e.g. hot, old, late).

He then asked participants to recall the words immediately after being presented with the list, then again 20 minutes later. What he found was that immediately after reading the words, participants found acoustically similar words harder to recall than dissimilar words. There was no difference between semantically similar/dissimilar words. When tested 20 minutes later, there was no difference in participants' recall between acoustically similar/dissimilar words, but there was worse recall for semantically similar words.

These findings suggest that short-term and long-term memory use different coding systems. Short-term memory relies on acoustic coding, on recognizing sound, so when words were too similar they interfered with memory. However, with long-term memory, the semantic similarity caused the interference. This is incredibly useful information for anyone who may be revising for a test or trying to remember important information over a longer period of time. Further research has shown that attributing meaning to a memory or piece of learning does indeed improve recall.

28

Developmental Psychology and Learning

Developmental psychology is the study of intellectual development, emerging personality, and the acquisition of language, as well as psychophysiological and social development processes as individuals develop from birth through to old age.

HISTORICAL DEVELOPMENTS

Developmental psychologists focused on theories of child development throughout the 19th and 20th centuries, during which period Charles Darwin undertook one of the first known studies of developmental psychology. In his short paper 'A Biographical Sketch of an Infant' he reflected on a diary that he had kept for 37 years, in which he had detailed the attainment of language and cognitive development of his infant son Doddy.

Child development, along with the development of language in mankind, was a significant part of evolutionary theory. In *The Descent of Man, and Selection in Relation to Sex* (1871), Darwin believed that children aged 10–12 months were at the same

Charles Darwin inspired the field of developmental psychology when he published his diary, which documented the development of his infant son Doddy.

level of language and understanding as dogs and wrote that language is not an 'impossible barrier' between animals and man. Darwin would go on to say in later life that he believed the first three years of life were the most important in human development. Darwin's article motivated others to study developmental psychology and there followed numerous publications in the journal *Mind*.

Developmental psychology originated as a specific discipline in a book called *The Mind of the Child*, written in 1882 by the German psychologist Wilhelm Preyer (1841–97). Inspired by Darwin's theory of evolution, Preyer used a rigorous scientific method to document longitudinal observations on the language development of his son, Axel, in the first three years of his life. Preyer analyzed the incremental growth of language, likening the process of brain development to the electrical wiring diagrams of the time. The book laid the foundation for the future study of modern human development.

Throughout the 1900s, behavioural and cognitive psychologists had become intrigued with the mind of the child and the variables of cognitive growth from birth to adolescence. Three key figures emerged during this time to develop their theories around variations of personality development and the relationship to upbringing. Jean Piaget (1896–1980) proposed a theory of cognitive development that established how children acquire knowledge and understanding of the world through four stages of development.

Lev Vygotsky (1896–1934) built on Piaget's theories to suggest that rather than cognitive development being solely about developmental stages, the environment the child was brought up in was also significant. Vygotsky proposed that vital to child development was the role of a significant other who guided the child through the learning process.

John Bowlby (1907–90) similarly looked at attachment and how a child's early life can significantly affect their adult personality traits, depending on their relationship to their caregiver in the first few years of life. While these three theorists approached child development from different perspectives, their theories continue to underpin most current research and collectively they inform the bigger picture of child development and developmental psychology.

IS DEVELOPMENT CONTINUOUS OR DISCONTINUOUS?

Continuous development is seen as a gradual change and improvement of existing skills and understanding. This would assume that development

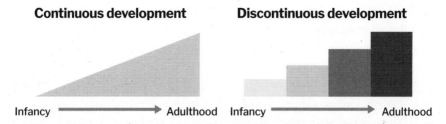

Continuous development **Discontinuous development**

Infancy ➡ Adulthood   Infancy ➡ Adulthood

Is development continuous, whereby we gradually develop, or discontinuous, whereby we pass through distinct stages?

continues at a steady rate into adulthood rather than occurring in discrete stages. However, there is some evidence, such as a child's ability to develop object permanence, that suggests that development can occur in abrupt stages. Developmental psychologists would also argue that not all children achieve these stages at the same age and that there will be variation between individuals.

Throughout our childhood and adolescence, then, there are significant stages of development that we pass through. However, into our adult life the process of development becomes more continuous. There are exceptions, though. As we grow older, the realization that we are limited in our time can cause us to reflect on past goals achieved or left unrealized. In some, this can cause an emotional rebellion or 'midlife crisis'. For women, the menopause causes hormonal changes that can affect behaviour. What is promising, however, is that in later adulthood even as we decline mentally and physically there is no observed decline in intelligence.

NATURE VS NURTURE

Does personality develop because of genetics or does it arrive from growing up in a certain environment? The nature debate seeks to understand how biology plays a key role in determining cognitive development. For instance, we inherit eye colour, hair colour and other physical traits such as height from our parents. Does it therefore mean that we also inherit behavioural traits? The nurture argument supposes that our personalities and cognitive development are shaped more by our environment. Experience informs our development and as we learn we adapt our template for the world around us.

The only way to study the nature–nurture debate effectively is through twin or adoption studies. Yet even these have many variables and it is hard to isolate the effects of either factor. There may also be epigenetic (a change in genes) effects passed down through the generations that impact personality development. Consider this: the egg you were made from developed in your grandmother's body. Therefore, environmental stresses such as war or famine that your grandmother may have experienced could have an effect on your development. This has implications for behaviour and personality development spanning different generations. This is a fascinating new area of study that takes developmental psychology back to its roots in evolutionary development.

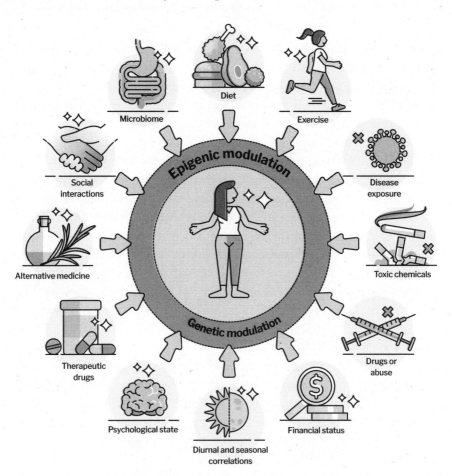

Your personality and development may be set by your genetics, which have been influenced over generations. However, environmental experiences also play an important role in the growth of your mind. Ultimately, it is impossible to unravel how much influence each of these factors has but they all contribute to making you who you are.

29

Social Learning Theory

Social learning theory was first proposed by Albert Bandura (1925–2021) in 1963. Bandura proposed that we learn how to behave by observing the behaviour of others, then imitating those behaviours.

MODELLING AND IMITATION

According to social learning theory, children observe the behaviour of models. Models may be someone a child knows, such as a parent, or someone they can observe from afar, such as a celebrity. Children next observe the behaviour of these models and memorize it. They then imitate the behaviour they have observed.

Although Bandura agreed with the concepts of classical and operant conditioning (see Chapters 11 and 12), he expanded upon them. He did not simply see people as passive learners responding to stimuli in their surroundings in the same way that these theories do. He believed that we are active participants in our learning – that we think about the link between our behaviours and their consequences. These thoughts mediate our behaviour and mean that we do not automatically imitate all behaviour we observe. They are called 'mediational processes'.

There are several factors that may affect the likelihood that a child will imitate the behaviour they have observed:

Albert Bandura, originator of the social learning theory.

- Whether or not the child sees the behaviour being reinforced. If they see the model being rewarded for the behaviour, the child will be more likely to imitate the behaviour. This is known as 'vicarious reinforcement'.
- If they can identify with the model in some way. They may be the same gender as the child, for example.

Transmission of aggression through imitation of aggressive models (Bandura, Ross and Ross, 1961)

The experiment described here is one of a series of experiments commonly known as the 'Bashing Bobo' studies. They aimed to investigate whether aggressive behaviours could be learned through imitation.

During the study, 36 boys and 36 girls between the ages of 36 and 52 months were recruited from the Stanford University nursery school. The children took part in one of three experimental conditions: observing a non-aggressive model, observing an aggressive model, or a control condition. The model was an adult experimenter unknown to the children and they interacted with a Bobo doll, a 1.5 m (5 ft)-high inflatable clown.

- Aggressive condition: After entering the room and playing calmly with some toys for around a minute, the model would begin to play aggressively with the Bobo doll. They would punch the doll, kick it and hit it with a rubber mallet.

- Non-aggressive condition: The model would play calmly with toys and ignore the Bobo doll.

- Control group: No model present.

Bandura et al. found that the children were indeed more likely to act aggressively towards the Bobo doll if they had witnessed the aggressive model. Children in the aggressive group imitated both physical and verbal aggression, whereas in the non-aggressive and control groups around 70 per cent of children showed no aggression at all. In the aggressive condition, boys were more likely to be physically aggressive than girls, although both sexes imitated similar amounts of verbal aggression.

Both the male and female children were more likely to imitate physical aggression by the male model. Bandura et al. theorized that this may be due to sex discrimination and gender roles. They noted that the children commented on male aggression by saying things like 'That man is a good fighter', whereas female aggression elicited comments such as 'That's not the way for a lady to behave'.

In subsequent studies, Bandura et al. repeated similar procedures with recorded aggression by a model. They wanted to test a popular theory that observing aggression on television was cathartic, and rid people of their own aggressive tendencies. However, they found that the children imitated filmed aggression, even if it was a cartoon, as much as they imitated live aggression.

Bandura et al. also repeated similar procedures to see if witnessing a model being reinforced and punished influenced the likelihood that the children would imitate aggressive behaviour. They found that children were less likely to imitate role models they saw being punished. However, even when no consequences were given for the modelled behaviour it was still likely to be imitated.

APPLICATIONS

This theory can be used to explain many human behaviours, such as how criminal behaviour may be learned. A person growing up around peers and family members who commit crime learn from these role models. They see the behaviour being reinforced in that the criminals may acquire wealth or possessions that they desire, and through this vicarious reinforcement the young person may be encouraged to imitate the behaviour.

30
Cognitive Development and Schemas

Born in Switzerland, Jean Piaget was a leading figure in the study of cognitive development and how knowledge is acquired in children. He would go on to develop fundamental theories of learning, incorporating both biology and psychology, which are still influential today.

JEAN PIAGET

As a child, Piaget was fascinated by biology and nature and initially studied zoology and philosophy at the University of Neuchâtel with a particular interest in epistemology. This combination of interests soon led him to work at the University of Zurich under Carl Jung, the famous contemporary of Sigmund Freud, and Eugen Bleuler (1857–1939), the famous expert on mental illness. In 1920, Piaget was working at Alfred Binet's institute, the Laboratory of Experimental Pedagogy, Paris, funded by the French government to investigate ways to help children who were struggling at school. Alfred Binet (1857–1914) and Théodore Simon (1873–1961) had developed one of the first standardizing intelligence tests (the Binet–Simon test) in 1905, which tested to see if children of the same age made similar errors in their reasoning. While Piaget was administering these reading tests, he noticed that there was indeed a pattern to the errors.

Swiss psychologist Jean Piaget.

However, he was more interested in the logical causes of the children's errors and asked them to explain their reasoning for giving a particular answer.

Through his research he understood that the children had used logical reasoning to come to their conclusions, but did not have the necessary knowledge and understanding to give the correct answer. Instead, they recreated their reality, filling any gaps in knowledge by using their imagination. This demonstrated important differences to Piaget between the thinking of adults and children and about how our logical reasoning develops.

Piaget continued to investigate how children reason. In 1921, he began to publish his research which aimed to take a scientific approach, building on the methods developed by Binet and Simon. His approach also included naturalistic methods, observing children from their early infancy, including his own three babies, as well as interviewing older children. From these observations, Piaget developed theories explaining how children develop what he termed 'genetic epistemology'. He identified three main areas of knowledge acquisition:

1. Knowledge about physical objects (physical knowledge).
2. Knowledge about abstract concepts (logical-mathematical knowledge).
3. Knowledge about culturally specific concepts (social-arbitrary knowledge).

PIAGET'S STAGES OF COGNITIVE DEVELOPMENT

Piaget believed that intelligence was not fixed, and that children undergo four stages of development to acquire knowledge about the world: sensorimotor, preoperational, concrete operational and formal operational stages.

His theory of cognitive development in children suggested that we progress through these stages as we mature biologically. All children pass through the stages in the same order, although Piaget never committed to an absolute age at which each stage should be acquired. This is because many factors influence cognitive development: culture, environmental interaction and biological maturity. Some children will not fully attain all the stages of development.

Stage	Age	Characteristics
Sensorimotor	0–2	Children learn by interacting with their environment. They learn predominantly using their senses. They begin to understand cause and effect relationships (if they drop something, it makes a noise) and they begin to develop object permanence (the idea that an object still exists if they cannot see it).
Preoperational	2–7	Children start to use language and symbols. They continue to be egocentric and focus mainly on their own needs. The end of this stage is marked by an understanding of conservation (knowing that objects can change shape or arrangement, but still have the same volume or value).
Concrete operational	7–11	A child is able to conserve (see previous stage) and has developed a strong understanding of cause and effect relationships.
Formal operational	12+	Children can now demonstrate abstract thinking. They can construct and apply hypotheses, and use deductive reasoning.

SCHEMAS

Piaget suggested that newborn children have a basic mental structure with innate behaviours that have been genetically acquired. As we progress through life we create little packets of information, called schemas, that help us explain and understand the world around us. He defined a schema as: 'A cohesive, repeatable action sequence possessing component actions that are tightly interconnected and governed by a core meaning.' We continuously adapt these schemas when we experience new situations using processes called organization, adaptation, assimilation and accommodation.

Organization is our ability to combine existing schemas and develop more sophisticated behaviours. As babies develop, they learn they can affect their environment, perhaps by moving a toy and use this information to grasp at food to feed themselves by applying their schema in a more complex way.

As we gather new information, we assimilate this into our schemata, updating our understanding of the world around us. If the new information contradicts the current model held by the individual we can experience disequilibrium. This can be disorientating as we struggle to accommodate the new, conflicting information. As it is incorporated into our understanding, we again experience equilibrium as our model for reality returns to balance. Schemas can relate to objects, but also experiences. For instance, we have a schema for how to behave in a cinema that is probably quite different to our schema for how to behave at a party.

We notice behaviour in children that fits this theory: when a child first sees a bat they may refer to it as a bird. They have assimilated their schema for a bird – a creature that's small, has wings and can fly. When you tell them 'No, this is a bat', they experience disequilibrium. Their bird schema must be incorrect or incomplete. They accommodate this new information and notice distinct features of the bat – perhaps the furry body or no beak. They now know how to recognize a bat, and can reach equilibrium.

31

Zone of Proximal Development

Lev Vygotsky (1896–1934) was a Soviet psychologist best known for his theories of social development, the foundation for sociocultural theory. He was influenced by Marxist beliefs and the Gestalt movement in Germany. He considered that child development resulted from the whole human experience, with more knowledgeable members of society instilling cultural values and problem-solving strategies through language and guided learning.

VYGOTSKY AND PIAGET

During his lifetime, Vygotsky received little recognition for his work and died at the young age of 38 from tuberculosis. Much of his work was suppressed at the time by the Russian government but his ideas have been posthumously translated into English and have received wide recognition. His work sits alongside that of his contemporaries, such as Pavlov and Piaget, to give us an important understanding of cognition and childhood development.

Vygotsky's ideas of development diverged from those of Piaget, who put forward the idea that children pass through a series of stages and that their development precedes their learning. Vygotsky thought instead that

Lev Semyonovich Vygotsky developed the concept of a zone of proximal development.

	Piaget	Vygotsky
Sociocultural context	Little emphasis	Strong emphasis
Constructivism	Cognitive constructivist	Social constructivist
Stages	Strong emphasis on stages of development	No general stages of development proposed
Key process in learning and development	Equilibrium; schema; adaptation; assimilation; accommodation	Zone of proximal development; scaffolding; language/ dialogue; tools of the culture
Role of language	Minimal – language provides labels for children's experiences (egocentric speech)	Major – language plays a powerful role in shaping thought
Teaching implications	Support children to explore their world and discover knowledge	Establish opportunities for children to learn with the teacher and more skilled peers

development resulted from social learning and that children gradually learn from parents and teachers. He went further, saying that development could vary between cultures, and that as well as society affecting people, people also affect society. For example, in pre-literate societies children will learn through storytelling or direct experience, whereas in Western cultures note-taking and revision for exams are used to memorize knowledge. Therefore, Vygotsky's theory allowed for this dynamic in cognitive development whereas Piaget had taken a much narrower view that assumed no difference in child development between varying cultures and societies.

THE ZONE OF PROXIMAL DEVELOPMENT

At the core of Vygotsky's theory was the idea that learning is a collaborative process whereby learners interact with their peers and teachers throughout their life. He noted that a child's actual developmental level, what they can achieve on their own, is different to their potential developmental level, or what they can achieve with guidance. He became interested in

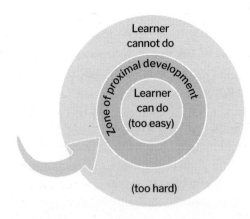

the reasons for this and posited that closing the gap between the two was where actual learning occurred. Vygotsky termed this concept the 'zone of proximal development' (ZPD or Zoped).

Vygotsky suggested that the ZPD is where learning will most effectively take place, with the more knowledgeable other guiding the student in the skills they need to be confident in the subject they are studying or skill they are developing. If the level of input is too low then students will not feel challenged and will make little progress. Conversely, if the challenge is too high, students will be unable to access and act upon what is being asked of them.

This leads into the second key principle Vygotsky identified, which was the role of the 'more knowledgeable other' (MKO). Essentially, this is a person acting as a skilled tutor who has a greater understanding of the topic, process or skill the pupil is trying to understand. They are therefore able to guide the student across the gap and help them move beyond their current level of understanding. It is also essential that the child is able to demonstrate their understanding, so there must be opportunity for a two-way dialogue between the teacher and student.

In an educational setting it is therefore important that a teacher acts as an expert, but also that they calibrate the level of teaching to suit the abilities of the individuals they are teaching. This requires them to regularly check the understanding of their students and adjust their instruction accordingly. This was a break from classical theories of child development at the time, which assumed cognitive development would have to take place before learning could occur. Vygotsky promoted the idea that learning and development take place at the same time and that 'it is through others that we become ourselves'.

Normally, the MKO is assumed to be an adult. However, this is not necessarily the case. The MKO simply needs to be a person who is more knowledgeable than the learner about the specific task at hand. It is also possible for the input from the MKO to take place at a distance. During the Covid-19 pandemic, many students were either taught directly over the internet or used web-based tutorials and software to guide their learning, assess their understanding and provide feedback on what they had learned. This demonstrates that in the modern context the MKO does not need to be an individual person as long as the key principles of instruction and assessment are applied.

THE ZINACANTECAN WEAVERS

An interesting non-Western example that parallels the concept of the MKO and ZPD is the process of learning observed among Zinacantecan weavers in south-central Mexico in the 1980s. Here, social guidance is very clear, with the women in the villages learning from a young age how to follow six basic steps while creating woven products. At the beginning of each step there is close involvement from the adults, who will spend 93 per cent of their time weaving with the child on their first garment. This has been observed to drop to around 40 per cent after the children have completed four or more garments and have become more proficient.

Similarly, the level of language used by the adult when instructing the child was observed to change over the course of their instruction. Initially, command words and instructional language were used in a clear

The Zinacantecan weavers in south-central Mexico were observed in the 1980s using six steps to create traditional woven products. Children are taught these from an early age, initially under close supervision, with the processes being modelled by an adult, until the children gain competence in their weaving.

and concise way. As the apprentice gained mastery of the processes, the language shifted to more open conversations about the various aspects of the work in hand. Similar processes have been observed in tailoring communities in Liberia and clearly provide a framework for learning skilled techniques.

LANGUAGE AND THE ZPD

For Vygotsky, communication and the development of language was an essential tool for cognitive development. He identified three types of language: 1) social speech or outward communication with others (from age two); 2) private speech that is inwardly directed (from age three); and 3) silent inner speech (from age seven). He suggested that initially thought and language were separate until they combined around age three.

Vygotsky was one of the first psychologists to focus on the role of private speech and saw the importance of this stage of language development. He believed that it allowed children to have a dialogue with themselves, operating as the more knowledgeable other, and rehearsing and planning strategies to problem-solve. Eventually, this would diminish around age seven as silent inner speech became the more dominant mode of verbal thought.

BRUNER AND THE SPIRAL CURRICULUM

In the 1960s, Jerome Bruner (1915–2016) built on the ideas of Piaget and Vygotsky and developed the concept of the spiral curriculum. Bruner assumed that children were capable of complex understanding and it was the constraints of language and teaching methods that placed limits on their ability to understand. Bruner devised the concept of the spiral curriculum whereby the basic aspects of a complex topic were taught first, then revisited in more depth later on. Teaching would therefore follow a pattern of gradually increasing difficulty.

He was interested in how knowledge was represented and referred to three different modes of encoding information into memory:

1. Action based (enactive representation).
2. Image based (iconic representation).
3. Language based (symbolic representation).

Bruner suggested that there was progression from enactive to iconic to symbolic representation of information when learning, rather than the intellectual stages suggested by Piaget. He stated that this was as true for children as it was for adults, and that rather than simply providing knowledge, education was about encouraging students as active learners and allowing them to construct their own knowledge.

To achieve this, Bruner devised the concept of scaffolding, whereby students could learn through discovery but were supported by the teacher. Initially, the teacher would closely supervise the students, jointly working through problems, then eventually removing the support, enabling the students to solve the problems on their own. This was a change from the traditional model whereby the teacher would act as an expert and 'tell' the students the information they were required to know.

32

Moral Development

We tend to think that all humans unconsciously adhere to a set of universal moral values. German philosopher Immanuel Kant (1724–1804) believed that there was a supreme principle of morality that he referred to as the 'categorical imperative'. Kant thought that 'truth of reason' is a moral law that all rational creatures are bound by. In other words, there is an innate moral code that all humans follow.

Take the 'trolley dilemma' for example. A runaway tram or trolley on a set of rail tracks is headed for a group of five people working on the railway line and will kill them. You can move a lever that would divert the runaway trolley on to a separate set of tracks. However, in doing so you will cause the death of another individual. Most people would reason that morally it is more acceptable to kill one person and save the lives of five. However, what if by intervening your action makes you guilty of causing the death of that person? Are you now responsible for their death? What if the 'one' person is a child or a member of your family? Very quickly, moral programming and decision-making can break down and there will be variations between individuals in how they respond to the scenario.

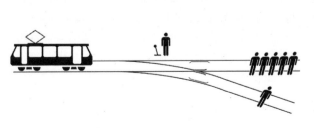

The 'trolley dilemma' is a classic example of moral reasoning. In this scenario, should you switch the runaway tram or trolley on to different tracks? You would save the lives of five people but kill another. Is it morally correct to intervene?

DEVELOPMENT OF MORALITY

Moral development is the process that children undergo in order to develop a sense of right and wrong within their society. Many psychologists have investigated the development of morality in children, but perhaps the first to do so systematically was Jean Piaget. Along with the developmental stages he established, he also connected moral development with cognitive development in children. Piaget saw that moral growth was a constructivist process whereby experience and action developed moral beliefs. As children get older, their ideas about moral judgements, rules and punishment change over time. Therefore, along with the stages of intellectual development, Piaget argued that there were also collective stages to moral maturity.

'Logic clearly dictates that the needs of the many outweigh the needs of the few.' Spock sacrifices his own life to save the crew of the Enterprise *in* Star Trek II: The Wrath of Khan. *But does logic always underlie our moral decision-making?*

LAWRENCE KOHLBERG

Lawrence Kohlberg (1927–87) worked to expand on Piaget's ideas and produced one of the most influential pieces of research into moral development.

Kohlberg's early life gives an indication of what he was to later spend his life's work investigating. In 1932, his parents divorced and subsequently the children were ordered by the courts to choose which parent they would live with. This moral dilemma left Lawrence and his other youngest sibling with their father, while the eldest children went to live with their mother.

In 1945, as a young man, Kohlberg again faced a moral dilemma while working on a ship smuggling Jewish refugees from Europe to British-controlled Palestine. This action broke the law and the ship was intercepted by the British blockade, resulting in Kohlberg being imprisoned. He later escaped with the help of the Haganah (a Jewish fighting force) and returned to Palestine to assist the Jewish refugees. Here, he renounced violence and instead took part in peaceful activism.

Kohlberg's fascination for morality stemmed from these early experiences, and when he returned to the USA in 1948 he enrolled at the University of Chicago to study psychology. While studying for his doctorate, Kohlberg became interested in Jean Piaget's research into the moral development of children.

KOHLBERG'S MORAL DILEMMAS

Kohlberg created ten hypothetical moral dilemmas and presented these in stories that represented moral problems. The stories forced a conflicting idea about two moral issues, and by studying the answers given by children of different ages, Kohlberg hoped to discover the ways in which moral reasoning changed as we grew.

Seventy-five Chicago boys aged between ten and 16 years old were selected for the study, and of these, 58 were selected to be followed up on every three years until they were 28 years old. Examples of the moral dilemmas included for those aged ten: 'Is it better to save the life of one important person or a lot of unimportant people?' and for those aged 13–24: 'Should a doctor "mercy kill" a fatally ill woman requesting death to put an end to her pain?'

After presenting the moral dilemmas, each boy was interviewed for one to two hours. Kohlberg was mostly interested in the reasons they gave for the decisions rather than the actual judgements that they made. He noticed that their reasons changed as the children grew older.

Kohlberg compared the results from the American boys to others from Canada, the UK, Mexico, Turkey and East Asia.

The 'Heinz' dilemma (Kohlberg, 1958)

Perhaps the best-known quandary created by Kohlberg was the 'Heinz' dilemma, which places saving a life in conflict with obeying the law.

The dilemma runs as follows: Heinz's wife is dying from a rare kind of cancer. There is only one drug that the doctors think might save her. A local chemist had made the drug. It was expensive to make, but the chemist was charging ten times the actual cost. Heinz only had half the money he needed to buy the drug. He therefore went to everyone he knew to borrow the money and tried every legal means, but he could not raise enough money to afford the drug. He told the chemist his wife was dying, and asked him to sell it cheaper or let him pay later, but the chemist refused, saying, 'No, I discovered the drug and I'm going to make money from it.' So, having tried every legal means, Heinz grew desperate and considered breaking into the man's store to steal the drug for his wife.

Kohlberg would then interview the children, asking them a series of graduating questions about the story, then analyzed their responses. The questions included:

- Should Heinz steal the drug?
- Is it actually right or wrong for him to steal the drug?
- Is the chemist committing murder if he refuses to give Heinz the drug?
- In general, should people try to do everything they can to obey the law?

Kohlberg was clearly influenced by his earlier experiences when he constructed the 'Heinz' dilemma. When he took part in smuggling Jewish Holocaust survivors into Palestine, he believed that he had a higher moral purpose than obeying the law.

KOHLBERG'S LEVELS OF MORAL REASONING

Kohlberg identified three levels of moral reasoning, with each level having two sub-groups:

1. **'Pre-conventional morality'** is the first stage of moral development. Up to around the age of nine, children's decisions are based on avoiding punishment and receiving a reward as they have not yet developed a personal code for morality.
2. **'Conventional morality'** is the second level, where upholding the rules of society has the highest value, as reasoning is based on the standards of the group to which the person belongs. Authority

and obedience have been internalized and often authority is not questioned.

3. **'Post-conventional morality'** is the final and highest stage of moral reasoning. Surprisingly, around only one in ten people are capable of the abstract thinking required for the post-conventional stage. These individuals follow a set of universal moral principles that may override the rules of a particular society or group. These moral principles are often ill-defined and based on individual experience. Typically, though, they include values around preservation of life and human dignity.

He found that children progressed through these stages in order, with each level of moral reasoning replacing the one before it. He also found that moral discussions helped children develop their moral thinking. Discussions between children at stages 2 and 3 result in the stage 2 child moving forwards.

Level	Stage	Moral reasoning demonstrated
1 Pre-conventional	Punishment and obedience	Rules are obeyed to avoid punishment
	Instrumental-relativist	Right behaviour brings reward
2 Conventional	Good boy/good girl inclination	Good behaviour pleases others
	Law and order orientation	Obeying the laws and being dutiful
3 Post-conventional	Social contract	What is right and wrong has been socially agreed upon
	Universal principles	Moral action is taken based upon an individual's own principles

Table showing the stages individuals move through as their moral reasoning matures. Surprisingly, the majority of people are not capable of stage 3 moral reasoning.

Kohlberg's study into the development of morality is not without its criticisms. It could be argued that the parents who signed their children up for the study were more likely to be interested in moral reasoning than the average parent. They may have had more discussions with their children about the morality of their decisions, which may have skewed the findings. Also, Kohlberg only investigated moral reasoning in boys. Subsequent studies in 1982 by his colleague Carol Gilligan (born 1936) found that girls and women reason differently, focusing more on interpersonal relationships. The study was also culturally biased towards those living in Western settings, where there is an emphasis on individualism.

However, Kohlberg has given us a fascinating insight into how moral values develop as we age and why, despite the development of morality appearing to follow certain levels of reasoning, it is subject to our understanding of wider social values.

33

Intelligence Theories

The only qualification needed to join Mensa, the elite society that includes only 'bright' people, is a high intelligence quotient (IQ). Mensa requires their members to take an IQ test and score within the top 2 per cent of the population.

They use one of many possible IQ tests in order to vet their members and as a result of using a repeatable, standardized test, they can be fair in their judgement and confident that anyone wishing to join the society has an equal opportunity to do so. However, the concept of intelligence and how to measure it is a topic that is continually debated in psychology. In this chapter, we will look at some theories used to define intelligence, and methods that have been used to measure it.

PSYCHOMETRIC TESTING

Francis Galton (1822–1911) introduced the concept of 'psychometrics' in the 1800s. The cousin of Charles Darwin, Galton was inspired by the concept that differences between individuals and how adaptive these differences are to a given environment are what guide the evolution of a species. Galton believed that intelligence could be the product of this biological evolution, and he attempted to measure it through tests of biological reflexes such as reaction time. By contrast, modern psychometric theories attempt to investigate intelligence as a group of mental abilities that can be objectively measured using standardized tests, often referred to as IQ tests.

IQ TESTING

Creation of the first standardized IQ is credited to Alfred Binet and Théodore Simon, two French psychologists who were commissioned by the French government to help students who were struggling academically and identify those who may need remedial help (see also Chapter 30). In 1905, they released the Simon–Binet test, which was used to see if children of similar ages made similar errors in their reasoning. Their test did not focus on skills that may have been learned through instruction, such as mathematics, but rather focused on more inherent abilities such as memory or attention span. The test was designed for children aged three to 13 years old, and was intended to provide a standardized test to compare subjects to average children of the same age.

Tests aimed at three-year-olds included questions such as 'Where are your eyes, nose and mouth?' or tasks whereby they may be asked to describe a picture. Comparatively, 13-year-olds were asked to complete a task more appropriate to their age, such as identifying the difference between two abstract terms.

The tests became hugely popular and their use was widespread. However, they were criticized for their reliance on the child's ability to complete tasks that may indeed depend on prior experience and tuition, and not inherent skills (also known as 'native ability'). For example, the tests were criticized for their over-reliance on a child's ability to use words and language fluently, their ability to read and write, and their ability to understand abstract terms. Binet himself did not believe that intelligence was fixed, and thought that it was very complex and could not be assessed using one single measure.

TWO-FACTOR THEORY

In 1904, Charles Spearman (1863–1945), a student of Wilhelm Wundt (see Chapter 1), proposed the two-factor theory of intelligence. He had noticed that people who performed well on one mental ability test tended to do well on others, and visa versa. As a result, he devised 'factor analysis', a statistical technique that examines patterns of individual differences in test scores. Spearman concluded that two kinds of factors underlie the individual differences in test scores:

1. **General intelligence (g):** General ability across a range of skills.
2. **Specific abilities (s):** Specific skill in one area, such as range of vocabulary or mathematical skill.

Mental ability	Description
Word fluency	Ability to use words quickly and fluently while performing such tasks as rhyming, solving anagrams and doing crossword puzzles.
Verbal comprehension	Ability to understand the meaning of words, concepts and ideas.
Numerical ability	Ability to use numbers to quickly compute answers to problems.
Spatial visualization	Ability to visualize and manipulate patterns and forms in space.
Perceptual speed	Ability to grasp perceptual details quickly and accurately and to determine similarities and differences between stimuli.
Memory	Ability to recall information, such as lists or words, mathematical formulas and definitions.
Inductive reasoning	Ability to derive general rules and principles from presented information.

While Spearman's theory accounted for an individual's ability to have one overarching general ability but also many possible task-specific abilities, it was still considered too simplistic by some psychologists.

PRIMARY MENTAL ABILITIES

In 1938, Louis Leon Thurstone (1887–1955) challenged the concept of general intelligence and introduced his theory of 'primary mental abilities'. Instead of viewing intelligence as a single, general ability, Thurstone's theory focused on seven different abilities.

INVESTMENT THEORY

In 1963, British-American psychologist Raymond Cattell (1905–98) also suggested that general intelligence could be divided, but this time into two parts: 1) crystallized intelligence and 2) fluid intelligence. Crystallized intelligence involves the use of prior knowledge, such as facts or processes that have already been learned, and can increase with age. Fluid intelligence requires no prior knowledge, but instead uses abstract thinking and logic. It also increases with age, but only until around the late 20s, when it begins to decrease.

For example, when solving a mathematical problem you may use your crystallized intelligence to recall times tables or symbols used in mathematics, but your fluid intelligence to problem-solve and work through the new challenge that has been presented to you. Cattell developed an approach called 'investment theory', which proposed that people with higher fluid intelligence find it easier to develop crystallized intelligence.

INFORMATION PROCESSING

These psychometric approaches to intelligence focus on the measurement of the capacity of intelligence. A different way to view intelligence is through the information processing approach, which focuses on the measurement of the processes involved in problem-solving.

Howard Gardner (born 1943) is an American psychologist inspired by the work of Piaget. Gardner thought that psychometric theories of intelligence were too limited, and that typical IQ tests only measured certain abilities, such as linguistic or spatial abilities. In 1983, he published his revolutionary book *Frames of Mind: The Theory of Multiple Intelligences*. In this book, he proposed that there are actually several abilities that could contribute to an individual's intelligence, and that these can be compared across cultures. According to multiple intelligence theory, most tasks involve a combination of several types of intelligence in order to be completed successfully.

TRIARCHIC THEORY OF INTELLIGENCE

A fellow American psychologist, Robert Sternberg (born 1949), generally agreed with Gardner that intelligence was more complex than comprising one general ability. However, he thought that some of Gardner's intelligences were actually talents that could be developed. He instead devised three different factors called 'successful intelligence', which make up his own triarchic theory of intelligence. This theory argues that intelligence is the ability to achieve success based on an individual's personal standards and the sociocultural context in which they live. As the name implies, triarchic theory (with 'tri' meaning 'three') supposes that intelligence has three aspects:

1. **Analytical:** The ability to analyze or evaluate problems.
2. **Creative:** Creating new or novel ideas. Requires imagination and innovation.
3. **Practical:** The ability to adapt to the environment, or adapt the environment to suit your needs.

CRITICISM OF PSYCHOMETRIC TESTING

Attempts such as those presented here to define intelligence can be necessary and useful in order for us to better understand the processes that underlie our abilities, to provide comparative measures of learning and to understand factors that influence learning and intelligence. However, there are inherent cultural biases that can occur when creating psychometric tests and attempting to define something as complex as intelligence.

Many psychometric tests assume certain knowledge and skills are possessed by those taking the test. However, as Jan Deregowski (born 1933) famously demonstrated in 1972, images are not perceived and understood in the same way by different cultures. For example, Deregowski compared three-dimensional perceivers – participants from Western cultures where three-dimensional images are often used to represent objects – with two-dimensional perceivers – participants from Zambian cultures who rarely used three-dimensional images. He showed them a drawing of an impossible trident and asked them to copy the image.

Deregowski found that the two-dimensional perceivers spent less time looking at the drawing and copied it quite easily. The three-dimensional perceivers, however, found it difficult to copy the trident. He believed that this was due to their knowledge of real objects interfering with what they know should be depicted in a three-dimensional drawing. The Zambian two-dimensional perceivers did not suffer from this interference because to them the trident did not look like a three-dimensional representation – it was simply a pattern of lines. This is one example of how assumed knowledge can influence tasks set on parametric tests, even if the task does not require specific factual knowledge or vocabulary.

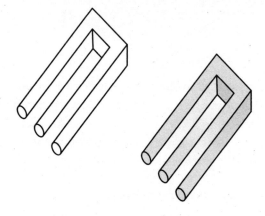

34
Human Intelligence

The previous chapter outlines the difficulty of measuring intelligence in humans, and these difficulties are compounded when attempting to compare human intelligence with that of other animals. While we cannot claim that humans are more or less intelligent than any other species, we can agree that humans have achieved unique feats of engineering and ingenuity that set us apart from other species.

Humans and other mammals also have larger brains than are necessary to perform the basic functions needed to survive, a trait shared with birds. But with large brains come drawbacks. They require a large amount of energy in order to function, and the large skull that goes along with them means that we are born early in our development and require more support from our parents than many other infant animals. The aim of this chapter is to discuss the biological and environmental factors that may have led to our evolution prioritizing these large and cumbersome brains and resulted in our unique brand of intelligence.

EVOLUTIONARY PRESSURES
Evolution by means of natural selection is a process by which those organisms best suited to survive in a given environment go on to reproduce and pass on their genes, and therefore also pass on the traits that gave them their advantage. The environment that led to a species having the traits it currently displays is known as the 'environment of evolutionary adaptedness', which for us and our ancestors was around 2 million and 100,000 years ago. During this time, what may have been adaptive for us could have been to find food, care for our offspring and build relationships with other humans who could help us to achieve these goals.

This meerkat demonstrates altruism by keeping a lookout for predators. Although this puts the individual meerkat at risk, it increases the likelihood of the survival of its closest genetic relatives.

When we consider our behaviour from this evolutionary perspective – that we strive for the survival of our genes – it can explain many modern behaviours. For example, it may explain why the most common phobias relate to creatures or situations that would have been a threat to us in our evolutionary past, or why we sometimes feel the need to 'fit in' and conform to group pressures. Being a social species, we have evolved to be predisposed to these behaviours.

Evolutionary theory can also be used to explain behaviour that may not seem adaptive for the individual, for example our tendency to be altruistic and prioritize the needs of others over our own. If we appreciate that 'survival of the fittest' does not refer to us as an individual, but to our genetic inheritance, we can see why it could be an advantage to sacrifice our own well-being in favour of our family or group. Altruistic behaviour results in your group overall gaining an advantage and your offspring or close relatives being more likely to survive. This trait can be seen in other species as well. For example, one meerkat in a group will remain on lookout and call to its family if a predator is approaching. The meerkat on lookout is much more likely to be caught by the predator, but it makes this sacrifice to ensure the survival of its genes, in the form of its close relatives.

MEAT-SHARING HYPOTHESIS

One theory of human intelligence that links to the concept of sociability is the 'meat-sharing hypothesis'. Rather than being based on the concept of altruism, it proposes that we shared this precious resource strategically in order to ingratiate ourselves with others and form alliances. In his 1999 book *The Hunting Apes: Meat Eating and the Origins of Human Behavior*, anthropologist Craig Stanford (born 1956) proposed that using meat as a form of currency to bargain and barter required intelligence, so those humans who were more able to keep track of their bartering and make strategic decisions in this way were more likely to reproduce and pass on their genes.

This links also to Byrne and Whiten's (1988) concept of 'Machiavellian intelligence', named after the Italian renaissance diplomat Niccolo Machiavelli, who famously believed that unscrupulous behaviour and deceit were necessary in politics. It is also known as the 'social brain hypothesis' as it does not entirely suggest that cunning and deceit were what played a role in the development of our intelligence, but rather social complexity. This theory suggests that intelligence evolved due to social competition over status and reproduction; those early humans who were more able to navigate the complexity of the society in which they lived were more likely to reproduce.

Food is not only thought to contribute to intelligence as a bartering tool, but the process of finding food may also have contributed to the development of our problem-solving abilities. In 2002, Robin Dunbar (born 1947) proposed that early humans were likely to be frugivores, or fruit-eaters, much like modern chimpanzees. As a result, they would have had to keep track of when each different fruit would ripen, how to tell when it was ripe, and plan ahead to harvest the food and manage their supplies. They would have had to travel further to find fruit that was ripe when they needed it. Folivores, animals who eat leaves, would not have to consider their food source so carefully as it would be more readily and abundantly available.

BRAIN CONNECTIVITY

Further work into how the biology of our brains may be linked to intelligence comes from brain scanning techniques. Haier et al. (1988) measured brain activity using positron emission tomography (PET) scans in participants when they performed an abstract reasoning task and a visual performance task. They found that both tasks activated the right hemisphere of the brain, but had different effects on the left hemisphere. Some participants with the highest test scores showed the lowest brain activity. This suggests that it may be the efficiency or density of neutral circuits that influence test scores, not brain activity itself.

Robin Dunbar suggested that much like modern chimpanzees, our ancestors may have used their intelligence to monitor the ripening of seasonal fruit.

However, studies of brain activity have been criticized for lacking precision. Neurotransmission, the communication between neurons, takes place incredibly quickly and would need to be measured in milliseconds to build an accurate picture of activity in the brain. PET scans like the ones used in this study often track activity in the brain over a 30-minute window of time. Even modern fMRI scans, which can track changes in the brain over a much shorter time, only measure blood flow. So while they may show where blood is being directed to and from in the brain, they do not track the actual activity of the neurons.

GENETIC ARGUMENTS

Despite the difficulty in measuring and isolating biological and genetic components linked to intelligence, there is certainly convincing evidence of a biological component. Twin studies can be particularly useful when investigating the role of genetics as they provide us with a way to investigate natural clones: identical twins. Researchers have found that identical twins have closer IQ scores than non-identical twins. It could be argued that this correlation is due to the twins' environment. Maybe they are brought up and treated in such a similar way that it is in fact their upbringing that is causing this similarity in IQ scores, although the effect is seen even when the twins are reared apart (Bouchard and McGue, 1981). This suggests that genetics played a greater role in the development of IQ than the environment in these cases.

In 2018, a group of researchers collaborating through the Social Science Genetic Association Consortium (SSGAC) analyzed the data of more than 1.1 million people of European descent. These people had allowed their DNA to be sequenced, and also provided data about themselves, including their educational status. This enabled the researchers to analyze the association between educational attainment and certain genetic markers, finding that genes associated with the brain development process and neuron-to-neuron communication were associated with higher academic achievement. Although correlations such as this should be viewed with caution and cannot explain why the association exists, it is interesting to note that the study found that 11 per cent of variation in educational attainment could be linked to genetics, whereas only 7 per cent could be linked to household income.

SOCIOECONOMIC FACTORS

Correlations have been found between environmental factors and intelligence test scores. Socioeconomic status and parental income have been found to influence the IQ test scores of children, with increased income correlating with higher IQ scores (Bouchard and Segal, 1985). It is difficult to separate genetics and environment in this way, when there is no way to identify whether the genetics of the person predispose them to a lower income or certain socioeconomic status.

The only way to be more confident would be to separate genetics and the environment, which can only be done by comparing people who have been separated from their genetic relatives and placed in a different

Identical twins can be used to study the interaction between genes and the environment. NASA astronauts Scott and Mark Kelly took part in a study on the effects of extended space flight on the body. Scott was monitored during his 342-day stint aboard the International Space Station, while his identical twin brother Mark was monitored on Earth. Comparing the twins showed which bodily changes may have occurred naturally, and which occurred due to being in space. Similar techniques can be used in psychology by studying twins who have been separated at birth.

environment, in this case, adopted children. In a study by Duyme et al. (1999), French children who were adopted at the age of four and had similar IQs at this age were placed into homes that were of low, middle or high economic status. The researchers found that nine years later all three groups of children showed improvements in their IQ test scores, but that there was a 12-point difference between the IQ scores of the children placed in low-status homes versus high-status homes. This suggests that the socioeconomic status of the adoptive parents, and therefore the environment that the children were raised in, certainly had an effect on the IQ test scores of the children.

In his 2011 book *IQ and Human Intelligence*, psychologist Nicholas Mackintosh (1935–2015) states that there are many environmental factors that correlate with IQ test scores – for example, parental socioeconomic status, complications at birth, nutrition, family size, birth order and amount of schooling. However, he makes it clear that these factors may not be causal, and that it may be that the child's IQ influences the parents' behaviour in some cases, or that genetics could still be linked to some of these factors.

35

Animal Intelligence

It is hard enough to compare measures of intelligence across human cultures with different values and priorities, so non-human animals present even more of a challenge. Animals may not display, or have any need for, the types of intelligence we value. To approach this question, we will look at some traits that many psychologists agree could give us an indication of the cognitive abilities of animals, such as brain size, self-recognition and problem-solving.

DISTINGUISHING INTELLIGENCE FROM CONDITIONING

It is tempting to see animals as being intelligent when they display human traits or perform entertaining feats. When animals are taught to perform, we may assume that they must be intelligent to be able to respond to their owner's requests. However, they are simply responding to operant conditioning, a learning theory we discussed in Chapter 12. Animals can also sometimes wow us with their ability to show problem-solving abilities that we usually assume are restricted to humans.

Clever Hans, for example, was a horse that became famous in Germany in the early 20th century due to his supposed mathematical ability. Clever Hans appeared to not only be able to add and subtract numbers, but he could also work out fractions. He would communicate his answer by tapping his hoof, so for example to give the answer four, he would tap his hoof four times. Hans and his owner toured Germany impressing the public. There was some speculation that Hans' owner, Wilhelm von Osten, was somehow feeding answers to Hans, but when Wilhelm invited members of the public to put questions to Hans he still answered correctly. The public were astonished.

However, when psychologist Carl Stumpf (1848–1936) and his colleagues investigated further, they found that Hans was indeed

Clever Hans the German 'thinking horse' being tested in Berlin, 1904.

displaying a form of intelligence, but not of a mathematical kind. They placed blinkers on Hans so that he could only see who was directly in front of him, and discovered that if he could see the person waiting for their answer he was correct 89 per cent of the time, but if he could not see them he only answered correctly 6 per cent of the time. Hans had learned to pick up on tiny cues from human body language and facial expression to tell when he was approaching a correct answer, at which point he would tap more slowly, then stop when given an unconscious cue that he had reached the correct answer by the questioner.

Hans was demonstrating a form of intelligence that may be very useful to horses, which live in herds: the ability to pick up social cues in the body language of others. We now know that many animals are able to respond to the non-verbal communication of their human companions, especially those animals that would naturally live in herds, groups or packs, where this skill would be advantageous. This is why when drug-sniffing dogs are being trained, both they and their handler must be unaware of where drugs are hidden in a practice scenario, so that their handlers do not accidentally provide the dog with a clue to where the drugs are hidden. It is important to remember when considering the intelligence of animals not to compare their abilities to that of humans, but to consider what forms of intelligence may be useful to them and their unique environment.

MACHIAVELLIAN INTELLIGENCE IN ANIMALS

For species living in large social groups, there are many potential cognitive demands. They may need to be able to recognize large numbers of individuals and tell them apart, remember where each member of their group falls in a hierarchy, and who is related to whom. They may also

The ability to perform tricks and seemingly follow instructions is not necessarily an indication of intelligence in animals, but rather the effectiveness of operant conditioning.

need to be able to form political alliances with other members of their group in order to improve their own social status, or even deceive others to gain an advantage.

One measure of animal intelligence that has been used by psychologists is Machiavellian intelligence. As mentioned in Chapter 34, Machiavellian intelligence describes an individual's ability to use cunning and deception, or even just an ability to manipulate a social situation in such a way that they gain from it. The theory is that intelligent, social animals will have developed the ability to manipulate and deceive others. Also known as the 'social intelligence hypothesis', this theory suggests that the increase in brain size during the evolution of species such as primates has been driven by the need to work in groups and make sense of complex relationships. Rhesus macaques, for example, live in complex societies. Their hierarchies are complex and long-lasting, involving social bonds between female relatives that can span generations. Individuals constantly compete for high social status and the power that comes with it using ruthless aggression, nepotism and complex political alliances.

TACTICAL DECEPTION

The ability to use tactical deception also demonstrates an awareness of the mental state of others, and so is considered by many psychologists

Rhesus macaques live in complex societies.

to be a measure of the intelligence of a species. Richard Byrne (1994) studied the mating behaviour of gorillas and found that subordinated males would 'sneak off' with fertile females that only the alpha male supposedly has access to. They thus increased the likelihood that their genes were passed on to the next generation not by using brute strength to outmatch their opponents, but by using stealth.

FORMING ALLIANCES

Another measure of intelligence may be the ability to form alliances, a skill that is likely to be more useful than physical strength when living in large social groups. Richard Conner (1997) suggests that in bottlenose dolphins, alliance-forming may be even more complex than that of any other non-human species, and suggests that the pressure to exist in complex social groups in which members are in social competition, but also rely on one another for support and protection, could be the cause of the evolution of large brains in mammals such as dolphins, humans and elephants.

SELF-RECOGNITION

A further method of assessing intelligence in animals is their ability to recognize themselves. Human babies and some other non-human primates develop this ability at about two years of age, but it is also seen in other intelligent mammals, such as elephants and dolphins. In 1970, Gordon Gallup (born 1941) tested this ability in chimpanzees by presenting individually housed chimpanzees with a mirror. He left them with this mirror for ten days, and found that after initially assuming that the chimpanzee in the mirror was another individual and reacting to it, they began to act as if they realized it was actually them. Gallup tested this further by placing a red mark on the brow of each chimpanzee while it was unconscious. He found that when no mirror was present the chimpanzees rarely touched the marks when they woke up, but when the mirror was present the chimpanzees quickly noticed the mark and reacted, touching it and even sniffing their fingers afterwards. This was a clear indication that they certainly knew that the chimpanzee in the mirror was indeed themself – they could recognize themselves as individuals.

This ability is not seen in many other primate species; even gorillas appear not to be able to recognize themselves in a mirror in this way. One issue with these tests, however, is that they rely on the animal caring enough that they have a mark on their head to actually react to it. Some species may simply not be vain enough! Gallup tested this idea by placing marks on parts of the body that were visible without a mirror, such as the belly or wrist. Other species of primate did react to marks that they could see without a mirror, suggesting that their lack of reaction to the mirror tests really was a lack of recognition.

What's more, while mirror recognition has not been seen in all primate species, it has been seen in other large mammals such as dolphins (Reiss and Marino, 2001), orcas (Delfour and Marten, 2002) and elephants (Plotnik, 2006).

TOOL USE AND PROBLEM-SOLVING

Until the 1960s it was a widely held belief that what separated humans from other animals was our ability to create and use tools. This represented a level of problem-solving and ingenuity that we believed was unique to us. However, we now know that many species, including other non-human primates, birds and even cephalopods, use tools to solve a variety of problems in their environments.

Jane Goodall (born 1934) famously first reported the use of tools by chimpanzees while she was observing them at Gombe Stream National Park in Tanzania. She observed chimpanzees using long grass sticks like fishing rods to extract termites from their mounds. The observation was so revelatory that when Dr Louis Leakey, Jane's mentor, heard about her discovery, he said that 'Now we must redefine tool, redefine man, or accept chimpanzees as human.'

We now know that many species use tools and show problem-solving abilities. Bird species in particular show a fantastic ability to problem-solve. Birds such as the New Zealand kea can solve simple puzzles on their first attempt, which suggests that they do not simply problem-solve by trial and error, but consider their tactics before solving a problem (Werdenich and Huber, 2006). When given a more complicated puzzle called a 'multi-action box', which has four possible solutions, one out of six of the kea tested found all four solutions, two of which involved the use of a tool to solve the puzzle. One out of five crows tested was also able to solve all four puzzles (Auersperg et al., 2010).

Crows have also shown the ability to complete 'metatool' tests, where one tool is needed to access another tool that is needed to complete a task, and the ability to modify tools in order to complete a task, such as breaking side branches off a stick so that it can be used to remove a worm from a tube (Bird and Emory, 2009).

BRAIN SIZE

Finally, it is a common misconception that brain size is an indication of the intelligence of a species. If this were the case, humans would be far from the most intelligent species, with our brains being dwarfed by those of larger mammals such as elephants or whales. What would be more sensible would be to compare the brain mass to body mass ratio of a species, because of course a large animal will need a larger brain to control all of the processes that take place to keep them alive. Human brains tend to account for about 2 per cent of the mass of our bodies, a much higher percentage than that of elephants and whales, whose huge brains are dwarfed by their equally huge bodies. However, the brain to body ratio of a treeshrew is the highest of any mammal, with their brains representing around 10 per cent of their mass, and some ant species exceed even this, with brains making up 14–15 per cent of their mass. Overall, though, the trend still holds that relative brain size does tend to correlate with animals that we traditionally class as intelligent.

Neuroscientists also argue that it is the organization of the brain that is as, if not more, important than its size. Humans have a higher concentration of nerve cells in the neocortex – where perception, decision-making and language are thought to originate – than any other species.

In summary, the issue is not whether or not animals are intelligent, but rather how we define intelligence in animals.

36

Attachment

The theory of attachment was conceived in 1958 by John Bowlby, a psychoanalyst exploring why children experienced severe distress when they were separated from their parents. Theories of attachment now encompass many different types of human relationship, and have many uses, including informing policies relating to childcare.

JOHN BOWLBY

Born in London to an upper middle-class family, Bowlby's parents spent only a small amount of time with their young son. Bowlby's father was a leading surgeon who worked long hours and who believed that too much attention would spoil a child. John was sent to boarding school at the age of seven, an experience that he found distressing and undoubtedly influenced his later career. Bowlby graduated in 1928 from Cambridge, where he had studied medicine and psychology, and volunteered as a teacher at Bedales and Priory Gate School, which specialized in children with behavioural difficulties.

After qualifying as a psychoanalyst, Bowlby served in the Royal Army Medical Corps throughout World War II. When the war was over, Bowlby produced a report titled 'Maternal Care and Mental Health' for the World Health Organization (WHO), which examined the mental health of homeless children in Europe. In it, he stated 'the infant and young child should experience a warm, intimate and continuous relationship with his mother (or a permanent mother substitute – one person who steadily "mothers" him) in which both find satisfaction and enjoyment.' This concept of the importance of a primary caregiver would be central to Bowlby's future theories.

Bowlby theorized that the earliest bonds formed by children with their caregivers have a deep and lasting impact throughout their life. Bowlby drew upon ideas from cognitive science, developmental psychology, evolutionary biology and ethology (the science of animal behaviour). He was influenced by the work of Konrad Lorenz (1903–89) whose well-known 1935 study on imprinting showed that during a critical period young geese would imprint on attachment figures in their environment.

Prior to the work of Bowlby and psychodynamic psychologists such as Freud, theories regarding parent–child interaction had mostly focused on survival of the child and the need to meet basic biological needs. It seems incredible, but before Bowlby's contributions, the importance of attachment in childhood had not been considered. Bowlby's theories filled a gap in explaining why parents are motivated not only to provide for their child's physical needs, but also their emotional needs.

THE ATTACHMENT BEHAVIOURAL SYSTEM

Bowlby considered attachment to be an innate drive that aided survival as the caregiver provides support, safety and security for the child. He argued that over the course of evolutionary history, a universal need had developed for infants to have close contact with their caregiver when they are threatened or under stress. Because these children were more likely to survive to reproductive age, these behavioural traits were gradually refined by natural selection and passed on.

Bowlby referred to this process as the 'attachment behavioural system'. It is an important concept as it connects the biological model of human development with our understanding of human emotion and personality development. Essentially, if the caregiver is attentive and in reach, the child is likely to feel loved, secure and confident. They tend to be more sociable, playing with other children, and will explore their environment. However, if the child perceives that the caregiver is distant or neglectful they will exhibit anxious behaviour including frantic searching, crying and clinging to the caregiver. This behaviour will continue until the child has re-established a desirable level of physical and/or psychological contact with the caregiver. If this contact is not possible, such as is the case with prolonged separation, the behaviour can continue until the child becomes emotionally exhausted. Bowlby argued that in the long term this could lead to a sense of despair and depression in children.

Bowlby understood that the attachment behavioural system was a generalized view and that there would be individual differences in the way children regulate their attachment behaviour. However, it wasn't until a colleague of his, Mary Ainsworth (1913–99), devised a systematic procedure to investigate parent-infant separation that a more comprehensive understanding of these differences was gained.

MARY AINSWORTH'S STRANGE SITUATION

In the 1970s, Mary Ainsworth developed a method of investigating attachment between a child and their primary caregiver. This method is commonly known as the 'strange situation'. Prior to this, attachment had been studied using more qualitative techniques, such as interviews and observations. In a famous study on maternal deprivation ('Forty-four juvenile thieves: their character and home-life', 1944), Bowlby had used interviews with caregivers and with the children, and reports from schools to identify whether maternal deprivation had played a role in the offending behaviour of 44 young delinquents in London. He concluded that maternal deprivation did indeed play a role in offending behaviour.

However, research such as this has the major drawback of being based on subjective opinion. Bowlby interpreted the observations himself, and could unintentionally have sought observations that matched his hypothesis. With Mary Ainsworth's 'strange situation' we have a way to remove much of this subjective bias.

Ainsworth recruited middle-class American families with children aged between 12 and 18 months to take part in her study. The procedures took place in a small room fitted with one-way glass, which enabled her to covertly observe the behaviour of the children. In a series of eight episodes lasting around three minutes each, a mother, child and stranger were introduced, separated and reunited. Ainsworth and her colleagues watched the reactions of the children and recorded specific behaviours they observed. She then used these observations to identify three main attachment types:

1. **Type B** – secure: The majority of children (around 60 per cent) in the 'strange situation' behaved in the way outlined by Bowlby's normative theory. When the parent left the room they became distressed, but actively searched for the parent when they returned and were easily comforted by him or her.

2. **Type C** – insecure anxious/resistant: Some children (about 20 per cent or less) were initially ill at ease, and became extremely distressed when their parent left the room. When the parent returned, the children were difficult to calm down, and often

showed conflicting behaviour by punishing the caregiver for leaving while at the same time wanting to be comforted by them.

3. Type A – insecure avoidant: A third group of children (around 20 per cent) did not become distressed when separated from their parent, and when reunited they actively avoided making contact with their caregiver. They instead focused their attention on playing with toys on the laboratory floor.

Later, a fourth attachment style known as 'disorganized' was identified, whereby around 7 per cent of children are fearful of the caregiver as a result of neglect or abuse. In this instance, the child is unable to place their trust in the caregiver and as a result feels unsafe and distrusting of adults. These children are referred to as 'fearful avoidant'.

The importance of Mary Ainsworth's study was that it provided empirical evidence to support Bowlby's theories of attachment. Children who feel 'secure' are likely to have parents who are supportive and sensitive to their needs, whereas anxious-resistant and avoidant children often have parents who are inconsistent with the care they provide and are insensitive to their emotional demands. This was perhaps the most significant achievement of the study, demonstrating the connection

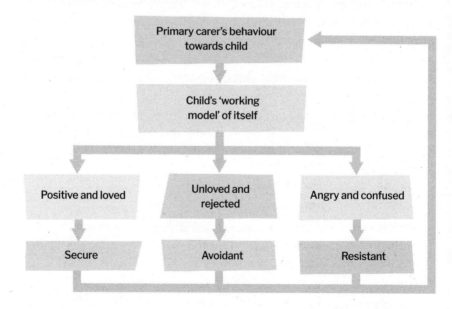

The internal working model is a cognitive framework consisting of mental representations for understanding the world, self and others. (Bowlby 1969)

between these behaviours and parenting interaction in the first years of the child's life.

The implications of attachment theory are far-reaching. The realization that a child could potentially suffer long-term consequences if they are separated from their attachment figure or the bond were disrupted during the critical early years of a child's life was an important step for Bowlby, and for a nation who at that time had experienced this kind of separation on a national scale, with children in the UK being evacuated from their families during World War II.

The application of these theories in hospital and educational settings has been a huge step forward in the intervening years, and we now appreciate the importance of care and emotional comfort being provided for children. This knowledge has also influenced policies, such as the need identified for early intervention when children are at risk of being left without a primary attachment figure, which has undoubtedly improved the lives and long-term prospects for thousands of children worldwide.

Affectional responses in the infant monkey (Harlow and Zimmerman, 1959)

In the 1950s and 60s, Harry Harlow (1905–91) and his colleagues studied how newborn rhesus monkeys bonded with their mothers, specifically whether the bond related to resources or the comfort supplied by the caregiver. This research gave support to the concept that early childparent relationships had a greater purpose than simply providing resources.

Sixty infant macaque monkeys were separated from their mothers less than 12 hours after birth. They were placed in cages with two artificial surrogate mothers. One was wire and had a milk bottle attached (providing resources but not comfort), while the other was cloth and did not have a milk source (providing comfort but not resources). The infants lived with the surrogate mothers

One of Harlow's rhesus macaques forming a bond with the artificial surrogate 'cloth mother'.

for at least 165 days. Harlow and Zimmerman found that after the macaque infants had gained food from the wire mother they would return to the cloth mother for most of the day to seek comfort. This suggests that the comfort provided by the cloth mother was a greater draw than the resources provided by the wire mother.

Next, the researchers separated the infant macaques into two groups, one group with the wire mother only and the other with the cloth mother only.

They found the infants all fed and grew at similar rates, but behaved quite differently. Those raised by the wire mother were observed to be more timid, had difficulty mating and related poorly to other macaques and were bullied by them, and the females grew to be poor mothers themselves.

Reassuringly, they found that if an attachment could be restored within 90 days, the effects were reversed. Only those kept without an attachment figure for longer than 90 days showed lasting behavioural damage.

37
Language Development

Language is a window into the human mind. The complexity of human speech is often credited with enabling the technological and social advancements we experience today. Shared knowledge and experience can span generations through traditional oral storytelling that is passed from adults to children, and through written language that can be stored and shared indefinitely.

Language is an essential tool in human co-operation as well as in expressing ourselves as individuals. Globally, there are more than 6,000 languages spoken and in every single human society studied by anthropologists there has been complex spoken language.

'Man has an instinctive tendency to speak, as we see in the babble of our young children, while no child has an instinctive tendency to bake, brew or write.' Charles Darwin

DEFINING LANGUAGE

In discussing the development of language we must draw a distinction between written language and speech. Although closely related to language, speech is different in that it is thought to be instinctive. In fact, while there is complex verbal communication across every culture, written language has only been seeded on a few occasions, beginning around 5,000 years ago.

Spoken language can be defined as 'a code in which spoken sound is used in order to encode meaning'. Quite how we learn language in our early years is a complex process, but it is suggested that there are four main areas of language a child must learn in order to gain competence. The first obstacle for a child is to learn the rules of sounds for their given

Captain Kirk may have been grammatically incorrect when he said 'to boldly go...'. However, the rules of universal language would judge his statement as being successful. Grammar and language are different subjects. His intention was clear and the sentence serves its purpose as a form of communication.

language (also known as 'phonology'), next is the meaning or semantics of words, then the rules of grammar or syntax, and finally a wider knowledge of the social context of language, known as 'pragmatics'.

STAGES OF LANGUAGE DEVELOPMENT

There appears to be a similarity across human societies in the sequence of language development, reinforcing the concept that developing spoken language is an innate process.

The process begins when a newborn baby is around one month old. Babies are capable of making an 'ooo' vowel sound when they experience pleasurable social interactions, as well as using different patterns of crying to signal their needs to the caregiver/parent. From these simple interactions a dialogue can begin to build between a baby and their caregivers, and patterns of behaviour and language develop around the daily routines, such as meal times and nappy changing. This in turn creates a 'shared rhythm' between the adult and child. These interactions also tend to take place when the parent and child are paying close attention to each other's facial expressions and eye contact. Through a process of repetition, an understanding of a shared language begins to develop, with both parent and child contributing to the process.

From the ages of six to nine months, frequent repetition of sounds such as 'dadadada' or 'mummummum', called echolalia, occurs. By this time, the baby is beginning to use some more complex combinations, such as vowel and consonant sounds. At around 12 months, a few first words may be beginning to emerge, but they may be misused. It may take another three to four months for the baby's vocabulary to develop, typically growing from 20 words at 18 months old, then rapidly increasing to 200 words at 21 months.

By 24–27 months old, most children are able to produce three-to four-word utterances and show some understanding of the grammatical rules of syntax. As children develop, they begin to use prepositions and irregular verbs, and they begin to reorder sentences to ask questions. For example, simple statements such as 'Maya and Isla are swimming' can be rearranged by a child to become 'Are Maya and Isla swimming?'

By around the age of three to five years, a child has grown a large enough vocabulary and incorporated enough grammatical rules to use complex language. It is even possible for children to simultaneously learn a second language, or even a third alongside their primary language. There may in fact be no ceiling to how much language the brain can accommodate, especially in these early formative years when the brain appears to be prioritizing this learning. It appears though that there is a critical period in early life when language development is at its maximum, and generally, as people age, their ability to master new languages diminishes.

LANGUAGE AND THE BRAIN

We still know relatively little about the mechanisms within the brain that are responsible for language development. What is clear is that there is a system of brain regions working together across both brain hemispheres to acquire and use language. Central to this mechanism (although not exclusive) are two specialized language areas related to the left hemisphere, called Wernicke's area and Broca's area.

Wernicke's area was first described in 1874 by German neurologist Carl Wernicke (1848–1905). He studied patients who could not understand what was being said to them. They were physically able to speak, but the words they made were meaningless. When his patients died, he examined their brains and found that they had lesions in an area located

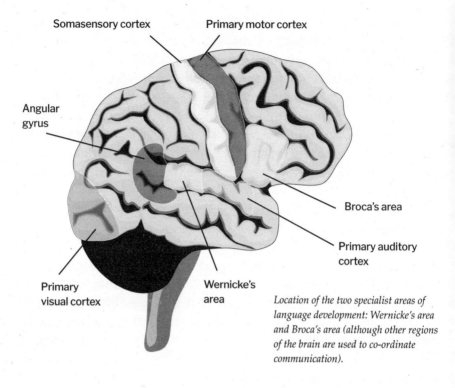

Location of the two specialist areas of language development: Wernicke's area and Broca's area (although other regions of the brain are used to co-ordinate communication).

between the temporal, parietal and occipital lobes. This area is now called Wernicke's area and is linked with language comprehension, integrating sensory information and co-ordinating access to auditory and visual memories.

Broca's area, discovered in 1861 by French surgeon Paul Broca (1824–80), is associated with speech production. It also regulates breathing patterns while speaking. It is responsible for co-ordinating muscles used for respiration, the larynx and the pharynx, as well as those of the oral motor apparatus such as the cheeks, lips, jaws and tongue. Damage to the Broca's area can mean that the person can make sounds but cannot form words. Some people with damage to this area of the brain understand the usage of correct words but are unable to speak, whereas others may be able to speak but use many incorrect words.

While these two specialized areas of the brain are central to language comprehension and communication, in order to be able to read, speak and write, other areas of the brain need to function in co-ordination. For example, to listen to someone talking you must use the auditory cortex, or to read a word you must view the symbols and then use the visual cortex to assimilate the information.

Everyday language and communication that we take for granted therefore takes a huge amount of neuronal and muscular firepower and is actually quite an amazing human capability. Theories for how language developed in humans is often hotly debated, not surprisingly as language is seen as the core of what makes us uniquely human.

BEHAVIOURIST AND BIOLOGICAL PERSPECTIVES ON LANGUAGE

B.F. Skinner argued that language is acquired through learned reinforcement. His theory of operant conditioning supposes that much like learning any new skill, language is developed through observation, imitation, repetition, errors, rewards and punishments (see Chapter 12).

Famous linguist and cognitive psychologist Noam Chomsky (born 1928) has criticized this behaviourist approach, and makes a counter-argument that the mechanisms of speech and communication are biologically determined and innate. Interestingly, in the absence of formal instruction, language development appears to follow a very similar pattern in children across vastly different cultures and backgrounds. It would appear, therefore, that we are born with an innate ability to develop language, based on a single master language.

Daniel Everett (1951), an American linguist anthropologist, further argues that spoken language may have developed as far back as 2 million years ago in our ancestor *Homo erectus*. Considered to be the first human species, these early hominins had big brains, walked upright, lived in groups and would have benefited from an ability to use language.

In 2001, a fascinating study described a faulty gene mutation in a British family known as 'KE'. About half of its members have severe difficulties with language, linked to a gene mutation called FOXP2. This is the genetic code thought to be connected to our ability to acquire spoken language. In the KE family, this mutation was faulty in the family members who had communication difficulties. Furthermore, studies into the gene mutation concluded that it was within the last 200,000 years that modern human-specific FOXP2 became fixed in the human population, time-stamping a date when human language likely emerged.

Interestingly, FOXP2 has also been found in other animal species. All bird species have very similar versions of FOXP2. The protein in the zebra finch, for example, is 98 per cent identical to ours. When researchers altered the gene mutation in captive zebra finches they were unable to construct a coherent song, demonstrating that FOXP2 was similarly affecting language development in the birds.

In a further twist, in 2008, Svante Pääbo's (born 1955) group at the Max Planck Institute for Evolutionary Anthropology in Leipzig, Germany, extracted DNA from the bones of two Neanderthals (a cousin of modern humans that is now extinct). Astonishingly, they discovered Neanderthal FOXP2 that carried the same two mutations as those carried by us.

This opens a deep and fascinating question about whether spoken language is uniquely human, and whether language could potentially develop in other species. For now, we can only dream of the conversations we might have had with our Neanderthal cousins.

38
Positive Psychology

Towards the end of the 20th century, Martin Seligman (born 1942) became the driving force behind the positive approach to psychology. This approach is based on the belief that we seek to enhance our lives and achieve a sense of fulfilment. It focuses on our psychological strengths and how we can nurture them, rather than on psychological illness or abnormality.

A FOCUS ON FLOURISHING

The concept of striving for self-improvement, virtue and self-awareness isn't new. Aristotle used the term *eudaimonia* to refer to the highest human good, and proposed that to live a good life a person should focus on a life of pleasure, political activity and philosophy. However, in terms of modern psychology many researchers believe that psychology has been dominated by a focus on pathology and understanding mental ill health or abnormality. They suggest that a 'shift' is needed in order to understand how people can flourish as individuals. This is the role that the positive approach intends to play.

'Psychology should be just as concerned with building strength as with repairing damage.'
Martin Seligman

THE ACKNOWLEDGEMENT OF FREE WILL

One deviation of the positive approach compared to many we have discussed so far is the acknowledgement of free will. Other approaches often take a deterministic approach, assuming that factors outside of our control influence our behaviour, such as our biology or childhood experience. The positive approach assumes that we have free will to make choices regarding our behaviour that are not ruled by internal or external forces. It would assume that you have made a free choice to read this book today and that your decision was not necessarily determined by external factors, for example prior behavioural reinforcement you had received for reading, or because you had been socially influenced by observing others read.

THE AUTHENTICITY OF GOODNESS AND EXCELLENCE

Another key concept in the positive approach is that goodness and excellence are considered authentic traits that are worthy of study. Seligman (2002) claimed that our view of psychology may be unbalanced, and that positive traits are as authentic and worthy of study as negative ones. The focus of this approach is on developing positive traits such as altruism and competence. It also focuses on the factors that contribute to a well-lived life, a concept known as 'the good life'. Seligman (2003) distinguished three different aspects of a desirable life:

1. **The 'pleasant life':** Pursuing positive emotions, and having the skills to amplify these pleasures. This includes doing things that make us happy in our day-to-day lives.
2. **The 'good life':** Identifying our individual skills and positive traits and enhancing these to enrich our lives. This could include having a career that enables you to play to your strengths, or using your skills to build friendships.
3. **The 'meaningful life':** Gaining a sense of fulfilment by using our strengths to contribute to the greater good.

Seligman suggests that by engaging in the pleasant, good and meaningful life we can find happiness. We can pursue these lives through positive connections to others, which allows us to build strengths such as loving, forgiveness and altruism. We can actively focus on and identify our positive individual traits, such as creativity, courage and humility.

Who is happy? (Myers and Diener, 1995)

In 1995, psychologists David Myers (born 1957) and Ed Diener (1946–2021) set out to investigate who is happy. They conducted a literature review of previous research on the topic of happiness. This included interviews and questionnaires measuring subjective well-being (SWB), observations, cross-cultural studies, and correlations. One prominent piece of research that they reviewed was a survey of almost 170,000 people spanning a variety of ages from 16 different countries (Inglehart, 1990).

Age and gender seemed to have little influence on happiness. People of all ages and genders were equally happy. However, at different ages, different factors contribute to happiness. For example, as people grew older their happiness was more closely linked to social relations and health.

Culture: There appeared to be differences in happiness ratings between countries and cultures. African-Americans reported nearly twice as much happiness as European-Americans (Diener et al., 1993); in Portugal, 10 per cent of people said they were happy compared with 40 per cent in the Netherlands (Inglehart, 1990); and people in individualist cultures reported greater well-being than in collectivist cultures. It could be argued that these differences may be due to the different emphasis each culture places on individual happiness and how this may influence responses to questionnaires.

Finances: People who are rich do not in fact report greater happiness. A survey by the *Forbes* rich list found that 37 per cent of the richest people were less happy than the average American (Diener et al., 1985), and people who win the lottery only report brief increases in their happiness (Argyle, 1986). However, money does become a factor affecting happiness when people are extremely poor or in poverty, and their basic needs for food and shelter are not being met.

The traits of happy people:

Myers and Diener found that there were certain traits common to the happiest people. They had high self-esteem, a sense of personal control and empowerment, were optimistic about life, and tended to be more extraverted and outgoing. The direction of this correlation is difficult to measure: it could be that people who have these traits are therefore more likely to be happy, or that being happy makes a person more likely to feel optimistic and outgoing.

Work satisfaction was another factor that affected happiness. Myers and Diener suggest that this is because our work provides us with a personal identity, a sense that our lives have meaning, a sense of community, and it provides flow in our day. Flow is the extent to which we become caught up in an activity so that other things matter less. People appear to be happiest when they are engaged in mindful challenges and experiencing flow.

Overall, Myers and Diener reported that people adapt to change and both the negative and positive effects of change diminish over time. People tend towards a generally consistent level of happiness. They also found that our cultural attitudes influence how we perceive events and therefore how they affect our happiness, and that having goals is intrinsic to happiness. Other factors such as finances are only relevant when they affect our ability to achieve our goals.

39
Mindfulness

In our busy lives we often rush through each day paying little attention to our current mood or the sensations we are feeling. We are so engaged in the flow of the day and what is going on around us that we lose sight of what is going on within us. Mindfulness is the practice of being fully present in the moment and having a conscious awareness of our thoughts and sensations.

MINDFULNESS AND MEDITATION

The terms 'mindfulness' and 'meditation' are often used interchangeably. However, there are in fact many different types of meditation and while mindfulness has some similarities with these ancient practices, it differs in several key ways. Mindfulness is a quality that can be developed and practised at any time no matter how busy you are, whereas meditation is a practice that is undertaken and requires dedicated time.

Jon Kabat-Zinn (born 1944), who founded the Center for Mindfulness in Medicine, Health Care, and Society at the University of Massachusetts Medical School, defines mindfulness as: 'Awareness that arises through paying attention, on purpose, in the present moment, non-judgementally. Mindfulness is used in the service of self-understanding and wisdom.'

So, while meditation has a greater internal focus on the mind, mindfulness encourages us to also focus on our external environment and sensations. Rather than closing the mind to external influence, it involves embracing and recognizing the external influence.

Furthermore, mindfulness can include meditative practices, but doesn't have to. It can be practised informally while undertaking any activity, such as mindful walking, eating, even showering. If while engaging in these activities you are consciously aware of your thoughts, you focus on the present and have an awareness of your sensations, you are doing these activities mindfully. Conversely, meditation involves formal dedicated practice and training whereby you are not engaged in any other activity. So while mindfulness and meditation complement and overlap one another in many ways, there are important distinctions to be made.

Mindfulness encourages good mental health by interrupting the constant stream of thoughts we experience and rooting us back in the present. When feeling anxious or overwhelmed we may allow our thoughts to take on a cyclical nature, continually reassessing the same thoughts and falling into unhelpful thinking patterns. By engaging in mindful practice we can recognize and acknowledge these thought patterns, but

Mindfulness can be practised anywhere you happen to be, whether in a peaceful room, a park, or, as here, on the edge of a lake.

also allow our mind to take a break from them. Mindfulness can be used by anyone to gain a deeper insight into their mental state, but has also been found to be useful in treating conditions such as anxiety or stress – it is now recognized and recommended by the National Institute for Health Care Excellence (NICE) in treating depression.

MINDFULNESS AS THERAPY

Mindfulness has also been applied in conjunction with other more formal therapies, for example in mindfulness-based cognitive therapy (MBCT), which incorporates mindfulness with the well-established techniques used in cognitive behavioural therapy (CBT). Traditionally, CBT attempts to modify people's unrealistic thoughts and beliefs, i.e. the content of our thoughts. MBCT aims to also alter the processes involved in thinking.

This technique has been found to be effective. For example, Teasdale et al. (2000) found that MBCT was effective in treating patients who suffer recurrent relapses of depression. In their study, 145 recurrently depressed patients were randomly allocated to receive treatment as usual (TAU) or TAU plus eight classes of MBCT. They then assessed their depression over a 60-week period, and found that MBCT substantially reduced the risk of relapse in those patients who had experienced three or more previous episodes of depression.

THE INFORMAL PRACTICE OF MINDFULNESS

Part of the appeal of mindfulness is how easy it is to begin practising it. In fact, you could start right now. Begin with your feet and focus on the sensation of your feet on the floor, or the material of your socks against your feet. Focus on this sensation for a few seconds, then gradually move your awareness up through your body, noticing any areas of tension, the temperature of your skin, any draughts or breezes rustling your hair. If any sounds disturb you, give them your full attention for a few seconds, then focus your attention back to your body. Similarly, if any other thoughts distract you, allow them to for a short period of time, then return to your area of focus. Remember that mindfulness does not aim to eradicate undesirable thoughts, but rather to allow us to recognize them for what they are and not dwell on them. This is particularly helpful if you find yourself fixating on past events, or becoming anxious about future events that are out of your control.

The accessibility of mindfulness is part of its appeal. You can practise mindfulness in this way no matter what you are doing; for example, if you are washing up you could focus on the temperature of the water and the sound of the crockery. However, to truly benefit from living mindfully you should practise regularly, and some people do engage in mindful meditation more formally, setting aside time each day or a few days a week to sit quietly and practise gaining control of their thoughts.

40
Applications

Applied psychology is the study of problems within human behaviour and the capacity to solve these issues. It can be a diverse area of study, including issues of health, counselling services, clinical psychology or even criminal psychology. The field of applied psychology builds upon the fundamental principles discussed in other chapters and focuses on the real-world application of these theories.

The evidence gathered by the basic theories is used in applied psychology to provide treatment for individuals for the issues they are faced with in their everyday lives.

CLINICAL PSYCHOLOGY

Lightner Witmer (1867–1956) founded the world's first psychological clinic in 1896 at the University of Pennsylvania. He published *The Psychological Clinic* journal in 1908, which documented ten years of research and educational experiments. With this publication he ushered in a new field of psychology and his conception established the course and direction of clinical psychology for the following decades.

At roughly the same time on the other side of the Atlantic in Paris, French psychologists Alfred Binet and Théodore Simon were developing intelligence testing for use in French schools (see also Chapter 30). The French government had become concerned about the inability of some students to cope with the schooling system. Binet and Simon thus developed the Binet–Simon scale, one of the first types of intelligence test for use in the school system, to help improve access to education for children in French schools.

Beyond education, other areas where applied psychology was focused included delinquency and improving industrial efficiency. The field

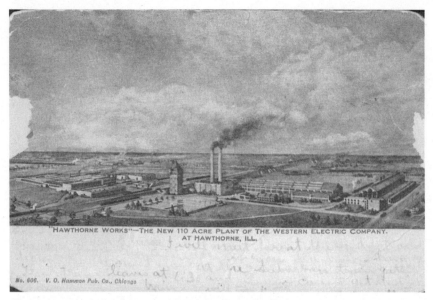

The Western Electric Hawthorne plant study investigated the effect of environment and social conditions on productivity. It became known for the 'Hawthorne Effect' whereby workers become more productive when supervised or observed by researchers.

of applied psychology therefore reflected the issues of the time and how to address the problems in society. Later, as concerns grew about how to treat the mentally unwell and prevent mental illness, the area of clinical psychology continued to grow and therapeutic approaches were developed.

This led to investigations into fear and aggression and how these influenced delinquency and criminal behaviour. John Bowlby applied his theory of maternal deprivation to a study of 44 juvenile delinquents (see page 169) to explain their behaviour. This was a step forward in recognizing how child development could impact individuals in their later life with potentially negative consequences.

British psychologist Hans J. Eysenck (1916–97), in *Crime and Personality* (1964) focused on how there can be a biological predisposition to aggressive behaviour in certain personality types. Although his approach has been shifted aside today, it was rooted in evidence-based practice and application of therapeutic principles. Treating these extremes of personality rather than just punishing them has no doubt had a positive impact on modern society, allowing individuals with personality disorders to function better in the world.

INDUSTRIAL PSYCHOLOGY

As technology has developed, applied psychology has had to respond to new pressures on the human mind and ways of working in society. For example, World War I caused military industrialists to call upon psychologists to investigate how to improve industrial output.

Studies between 1929 and 1932 at Western Electric's Hawthorne plant near Chicago by Elton Mayo (1880–1949) investigated the working environment as well as employee selection and management in order to improve industrial output. Frederick Taylor (1856–1915) also looked at factory design to increase productivity. However, these approaches were often seen as being at the expense of employee well-being.

Lillian Gilbreth (1878–1972) was interested in time and motion studies and how reducing the number of actions made by a worker could improve productivity. She researched time management, stress and employee fatigue. In 1914, she wrote the book *The Psychology of Management: The Function of the Mind in Determining, Teaching, and Installing Methods of Least Waste*, which was highly influential in organizing the workplace. Her ideas are still found in everyday life, from the idea of putting shelves inside refrigerator doors to the pedal-operated rubbish bin.

Around the same time, in 1915, Eleanor Clarke Slagle (1870–1942) organized the first educational programme for occupational therapists, therefore legitimizing applied psychology in the workplace.

Lillian Gilbreth, who is credited with inventing the pedal bin after her time and motion study in the workplace. Her influential research formed the cornerstone of industrial management from 1914 to the present day.

SPACE PSYCHOLOGY

By the end of World War II, manned space flight was on the horizon. Engineers were concerned about the extreme physical effects and isolation of space flight on the pilots who were to become the first astronauts. NASA thus used the techniques for industrial selection and management and took them to a new level. Astronauts were subjected to psychometric testing that investigated stress responses, group behaviour and problem-solving skills to determine if applicants had 'The Right Stuff'. Seven fighter pilots were selected for the *Mercury* programme from this testing regime including Alan Shepard. He was to become the first American in space and later flew to the Moon.

However, NASA had to rethink its selection process since on Shepard's *Apollo 14* mission, he smuggled a golf club on board and became the first person to play golf on the Moon. Unfortunately, this action was at the expense of collecting vital rock samples or sending a geologist (which they only did on the final mission) to carry out vital scientific work.

Moving forward, it was clear to NASA that they needed to change their selection process and look beyond the 'fighter jocks' to crew their

Commander of Apollo 14 *Alan Shepard playing golf on the Moon. NASA selected its astronauts based on their military backgrounds and capabilities as fighter pilots, which author Tom Wolfe coined 'The Right Stuff'. Modern missions select crew with 'The Right Mix', whereby astronauts have a broader range of scientific and interpersonal skills, which are required for the International Space Station (ISS) and deep space missions.*

future missions. With NASA now looking to Mars and deep space flight, they wanted to select crews based on isolation and group dynamics. What followed was a series of fascinating experiments in the Biosphere projects in the late 1980s and early 1990s, which resulted in divisions in the groups and a complete social breakdown. This demonstrated to NASA that the psychological problems of getting to Mars were perhaps greater than the technical engineering challenges of a future mission.

APPLICATIONS OF PSYCHOLOGY

Applied psychology therefore has a broad range of fascinating areas, from the workplace and everyday life, understanding criminal behaviour, and preparing for the different futures that lie ahead of human society. The approaches are informed by the theories developed in the 19th and 20th centuries, applying theories of biological, psychodynamic, behavioural and cognitive approaches to real-world issues. The following chapters contain a selection of some of the key areas in which multiple branches of psychology have been applied to explain specific behaviours, for example stress, isolation and criminal behaviours.

41
Stress

American physiologist Walter Cannon (1871–1945) is considered to be the first person to study the body's physiological reaction to stress. At the start of the 20th century, he proposed that the changes we notice in our body when we come into contact with something that we perceive to be a threat, for example increased heart rate or heavy breathing, were due to something he called the 'fight or flight' response.

Although we usually consider stress a negative emotion, our physical reaction to stress is actually adaptive. It would have helped our ancestors to be physically ready to confront the stressors in their environment by preparing their bodies to fight, run or chase. Now, many of the stressors we encounter cannot be solved with a physical reaction and this stress response that has served us so well has become a hindrance in some circumstances. In this chapter, we will look in more detail at our biological reaction to stress, how society contributes to our experience of stress, and how differences between us mean that we respond to stress in different ways.

TYPES OF STRESS
Most forms of stress can be placed in one of three categories, and each can affect us in a different way:

1. **Acute stress:** This is the most commonly recognized form of stress. It refers to immediate stressors that are usually discrete events, for example an upcoming deadline at work or an exam.
2. **Episodic acute stress:** These are repeated instances of short-term stress. For example, being stuck in traffic on your way to work.

3. **Chronic stress:** This persists over long periods of time. It may be
   caused by stressors that are difficult to manage and so difficult
   to resolve. Examples include poverty or persistent relationship
   problems, which leave the individual feeling that there is no way
   out.

We have different physiological reactions depending on whether we are
suffering from short-term (acute) stress, or long-term (chronic) stress.

BIOLOGICAL EFFECTS OF SHORT-TERM STRESS
Short-term stress activates a biological system called the sympathomedullary
pathway, which begins in the hypothalamus and results in our body
releasing hormones to induce the fight or flight response. The hypothalamus
is a small area in the centre of the brain that regulates bodily conditions
such as temperature, and also controls the release of hormones. When
the hypothalamus detects a stressor in our environment, it signals the
sympathetic nervous system to communicate with the adrenal medulla,
a part of the adrenal gland above the kidney. The adrenal medulla then

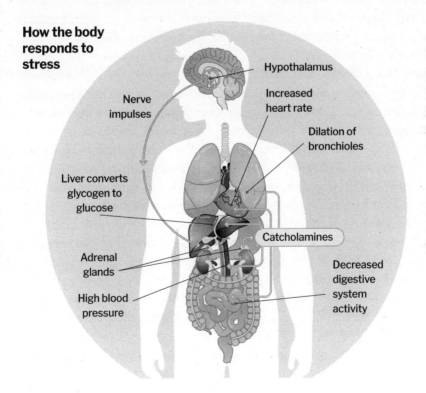

How the body responds to stress

Hypothalamus

Nerve impulses

Increased heart rate

Dilation of bronchioles

Liver converts glycogen to glucose

Catecholamines

Adrenal glands

High blood pressure

Decreased digestive system activity

releases the hormones adrenaline and noradrenaline into the bloodstream, and they stimulate the physical responses we associate with immediate shock or stress, such as an increased heart rate, a rise in blood pressure and dilated pupils.

BIOLOGICAL EFFECTS OF LONG-TERM STRESS

During longer-term, chronic stress it is the hypothalamic pituitary adrenal system that is activated. It also begins with the hypothalamus recognizing a stressor and activating the endocrine (hormonal) system. However, instead of communicating with the adrenal medulla it instead activates the adrenal cortex, the outer part of the adrenal gland. This then releases the hormone cortisol into the bloodstream. This affects the body by releasing stored glucose from the liver and suppressing the immune system.

In the long term, these responses can have significant negative effects on our health. With a suppressed immune system we are more likely to fall ill, and changes in steroid hormones such as cortisol are associated with difficulties with memory. However, in our evolutionary past it is believed that this response to chronic stress was still useful to us. It releases energy stores and is thought to lower our sensitivity to pain, possibly allowing us to continue to function in the aftermath of a stressful event.

THE TRANSACTIONAL MODEL

The physiological reactions to stress ultimately rely on our brain perceiving a situation as a stressor. There are some innate reactions that induce a stress response, such as hearing a loud bang, which sets our heart beating, but others depend on our perception of the event as being stressful.

To explain this, in 1984, Richard Lazarus (1922–2002) and Susan Folkman (born 1938) introduced the 'transactional model', which emphasizes stress as an interaction between a person and their environment. A person may make a primary appraisal of the situation, considering whether or not a threat is significant. For example, the risk of your car breaking down may not be very significant if you work from home and have a second car in your household, but it may be very significant if you commute to work and it is your only means of transport. Then a secondary appraisal is made, whereby they judge whether or not they have the resources available to handle the threat. For example, do they have the money to get the car fixed, or the knowledge and time to fix it themselves? The transactional model proposes that stress is a 'lack of fit' between the

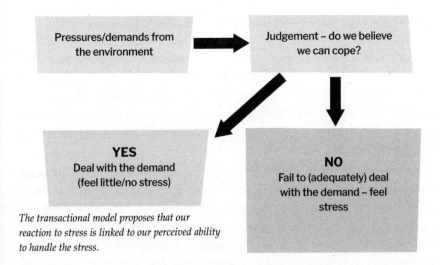

| Pressures/demands from the environment | → | Judgement – do we believe we can cope? |

YES
Deal with the demand
(feel little/no stress)

NO
Fail to (adequately) deal with the demand – feel stress

The transactional model proposes that our reaction to stress is linked to our perceived ability to handle the stress.

perceived demands of the environment and an individual's perceived ability to cope with these demands.

LIFE CHANGES AND DAILY HASSLES

As well as our perception of the stressor having an impact on our response, the nature of the stressor itself also plays a part. Holmes and Rahe were doctors who noticed that people they were treating for various illnesses had experienced many significant life events in the two years prior to becoming ill. In 1967, they set about creating a questionnaire to measure these life events.

Holmes and Rahe created a list of 43 events – including things such as divorce, death of a spouse, Christmas and holidays – and planned to assign each one a score, known as a 'life change unit'. They assigned marriage an arbitrary baseline score of 50 then asked 394 people to rate each of the other life events against it, giving them a score based on whether they were more or less stressful.

They then used the results to develop a questionnaire called the Social Readjustment Rating Scale (SRRS). Events that are considered most stressful, such as the death of a spouse or divorce, were given a high number. Less stressful events such as Christmas or a holiday have a lower number. Their intention was that a person could complete the questionnaire then add up their score to get a judgement regarding how many life events they are currently experiencing, and therefore how much stress they are managing.

What is significant about the SRRS is that it includes events that are perceived as pleasant, for example Christmas or getting married, but acknowledges that they too can be a source of accumulated stress. Holmes and Rahe did indeed find that there was a correlation between life events and illness. In a 1970 survey of 2,684 naval staff taken before and during a six- to eight-month tour of duty, they found that the higher a person scored on the SRRS the more likely they were to suffer illness during their tour.

However, there is some argument that it is not the large live events that have the biggest impact on our health. They tend to be discrete one-off events that subside in time. Furthermore, when a significant life event occurs we often receive support from friends or family, or can at least receive some acknowledgement socially that what we are experiencing is challenging. What may have a more cumulative negative effect on our health are those stressors that, however minor, happen continuously and go both unnoticed and unsupported. In other words, daily hassles. Daily hassles may include events such as losing your keys, being stuck in traffic or running out of biscuits.

According to Lazarus et al. (1980), these can be counterbalanced by uplifts. These are events that make us feel good, such as having a good night's sleep or receiving a compliment, and they give us a break from the daily hassles. Kanner et al. (1981) designed a questionnaire to measure hassles and uplifts, and found that their hassles and uplifts scale correlated more closely than the SRRS with people having stress-related problems, such as anxiety and depression.

THE HARDY PERSONALITY

As well as the nature of the event itself, there is also the impact of our personality to consider when discussing our response to stress. Suzanne Kobasa introduced the concept of hardiness and the 'hardy personality'. In 1979, Kobasa studied business executives, all of whom reported high levels of stressful life events in the previous three years. She found that those who reported low levels of illness following these life events had hardier personalities than those who reported illness. They rated highly on control, commitment and challenge. Kobasa suggested that for hardy people, stressors have less of a psychological and physical impact. A hardy personality 'buffers' against the negative effects of stressful situations and is comprised of three elements:

1. **Control:** A hardy person believes they can influence events and are in charge of their environment.
2. **Commitment:** They meet challenges rather than avoiding them.
3. **Challenge:** Hardy people view stressors as challenges to be met rather than as a threat.

Therefore, if hardy people do not perceive life events as being stressful but rather as challenges that can be overcome, then their physical stress response will be reduced and its negative health consequences less severe.

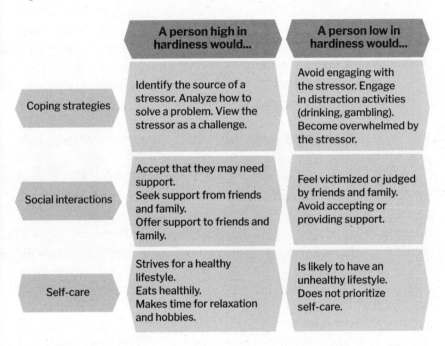

	A person high in hardiness would...	A person low in hardiness would...
Coping strategies	Identify the source of a stressor. Analyze how to solve a problem. View the stressor as a challenge.	Avoid engaging with the stressor. Engage in distraction activities (drinking, gambling). Become overwhelmed by the stressor.
Social interactions	Accept that they may need support. Seek support from friends and family. Offer support to friends and family.	Feel victimized or judged by friends and family. Avoid accepting or providing support.
Self-care	Strives for a healthy lifestyle. Eats healthily. Makes time for relaxation and hobbies.	Is likely to have an unhealthy lifestyle. Does not prioritize self-care.

PERSONALITY TYPE

Another aspect of personality that may affect our reaction to stress was first introduced by Meyer Friedman (1910–2001) and Ray Rosenman. The cardiologists studied their patients and noticed that some were unable to sit calmly in the waiting room – they sat on the edges of their seats and leaped up frequently rather than sitting in a relaxed state. The two doctors labelled this behaviour 'type A personality'. The theory now encompasses three personality types – A, B and C – and it is believed that they exist on a continuum rather than being discrete personality types.

The concept was first introduced when in 1976 Friedman and Rosenman published the results of a longitudinal study that they conducted over a period of eight-and-a-half years. Friedman and Rosenman surveyed 3,154 middle-aged, male managers and executives using questionnaires that included questions such as:

- Do you feel guilty if you use spare time to relax?
- Do you need to win in order to derive enjoyment from games and sports?
- Do you generally move, walk and eat rapidly?
- Do you often try to do more than one thing at a time?

They also asked the questions in such a way that it would elicit a stress response from type A participants, for example talking slowly. From

Type A Individuals	Type B Individuals

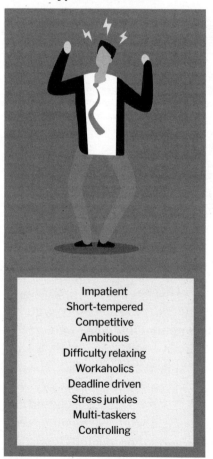

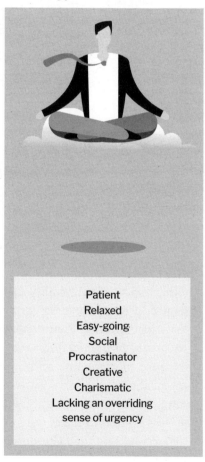

Type A Individuals	Type B Individuals
Impatient	Patient
Short-tempered	Relaxed
Competitive	Easy-going
Ambitious	Social
Difficulty relaxing	Procrastinator
Workaholics	Creative
Deadline driven	Charismatic
Stress junkies	Lacking an overriding
Multi-taskers	sense of urgency
Controlling	

the participants' responses and the experimenters' observations, each participant was put into one of three groups:

1. **Type A behaviour:** Competitive, ambitious, impatient, aggressive, fast-talking.
2. **Type B behaviour:** Relaxed, non-competitive.
3. **Type C behaviour:** 'Nice,' hard-working but become apathetic when faced with stress.

Eight years later, 257 of the participants had developed coronary heart disease. Of these 257 men, 70 per cent had been identified as type A personalities. The concept of personality types is further evidence of the possible link between our psychological reaction to stress and the physical repercussions of experiencing stressful situations. Our reaction to stress is clearly a complicated interaction between our perception and our physiology.

42

Isolation

Towards the end of 2019, the World Health Organization received reports of a cluster of unexplained pneumonia cases in East Asia. Within a matter of months, Covid-19 had spread globally. Governments scrambled to deal with the pace of the emerging pandemic as the novel virus spread. Throughout the world preparations were made for an unprecedented lockdown of the public to slow the spread of the virus. This would lead to millions living in a form of semi-isolation for months over the coming year.

In the lead-up to the lockdown, many psychologists feared the impact that this self-isolation could have on the mental health of the population. The effects of isolation had long been studied and had shown that it increases physical health problems and reduces life expectancy. There was also an expectation that anxiety and depression would increase en masse, particularly in vulnerable adult groups who were already experiencing loneliness and lacked support networks. Self-isolation was thus viewed as a necessary but costly decision.

However, as we will see, despite being a social species, our reactions to isolation vary based on multiple factors, and our ability to adapt means that we can in fact be surprisingly resilient when faced with extended periods of isolation.

PERSPECTIVES ON ISOLATION

Although many of us live alone and may choose to spend time by ourselves, prolonged isolation is relatively unusual. However, there are some cases where individuals have psychological conditions that cause them to become isolated. Depression may cause people to withdraw, and socially anxious people may choose to avoid social situations as

A woman eats alone on her balcony during the first Covid-19 lockdown in Italy in early 2020.

they find them stressful and unpleasant experiences. Other individuals may display social anhedonia, an extreme personality type whereby the person gains little or no pleasure from contact with others and is genuinely uninterested in engaging with other people.

While the previous examples stem from a negative psychological state, there are also people who have been described as 'happy introverts'. These are people who are psychologically healthy and enjoy their own company for positive reasons. They may benefit from isolation from other people by exploring their spirituality, or they may find that they are more creative when by themselves and encouraged to explore their own imagination. These positive effects of solitude are often overlooked in discussions surrounding isolation, the difference perhaps being that they are instances of self-selected isolation, rather than enforced isolation.

RESEARCHING ISOLATION

Some of the first studies into isolation came about in the 1950s. They coincided with fears of communist brainwashing techniques and isolation being used against Western prisoners in the Korean War. The McGill University in Montreal, Canada was the first to carry out official laboratory research into isolation.

During the study, volunteers at the university were deprived of sensory input and held in isolation. At the beginning of the experiment, researchers found that the participants slept a lot, but as time progressed they became bored and then agitated. They began making noises and found it hard to concentrate or focus on the tasks that they had been given to complete, such as recalling numbers. In extreme cases, some of the volunteers reported seeing hallucinations.

Most of the volunteers could not tolerate the conditions and were unable to maintain isolation beyond three days. These experiments proved to be controversial and in some cases researchers involved in the experiments were attacked by political activists, who associated the experiments with the actions of the CIA and the deep state. There were clearly limitations to these experiments, but it was evident that one of the main challenges of isolation is dealing with tedium and monotony.

EXAMPLES OF EXTREME ISOLATION

For hundreds of years, seafarers and explorers have had to deal with long voyages and prolonged isolation, being separated from society in small groups rather than as individuals. Antarctica is perhaps the loneliest place on Earth with no indigenous human population, extreme cold and situated thousands of miles in all directions from any other land mass. During Ernest Shackleton's 1908 expedition to Antarctica, the crew entertained themselves with music, theatrical performances and cultural celebrations. They spent hours preparing food, and dining was an important fixture of the daily routine. Crews in Antarctica have also been observed to drink and smoke more to cope with the solitude and monotony they experience, particularly over the long Antarctic winter.

During Shackleton's second expedition to Antarctica, the crew became marooned for four-and-a-half months on Elephant Island. Running out of tobacco, in their desperation they smoked penguin feathers and pieces of wood. When the rescue party returned, they threw bags of tobacco onshore before they even landed to pick up the stranded sailors.

During the Covid-19 lockdown, similar trends were observed, with research showing nearly half of respondents had gained weight through increased eating and inactivity, and one-third had seen their alcohol consumption increasing. Isolation can lead us to make choices that can affect our physical health in order to preserve our mental well-being in an attempt to protect ourselves from the potentially damaging psychological impacts of being alone.

THE EFFECTS OF LONG-TERM ISOLATION

Michel Siffre (born 1939), who conducted the biorhythm experiments described in Chapter 43, experienced extreme isolation on multiple occasions. In one of the final experiments he took part in, Siffre spent six months in a chamber 134 m (440 ft) from the entrance to the Midnight Cave system in Texas. He took with him a selection of books and a record

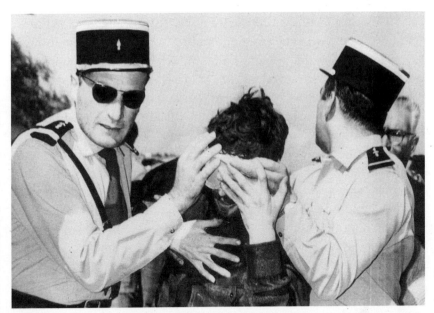

Michel Siffre emerges from one of his stints in isolation. In this photo, taken on 19 September 1962, he has just spent nine weeks alone in a cave 122 m (400 ft) underground in southern France. His eyes are covered to protect them from the light.

player to pass the time. However, the conditions in the cave caused the record player to break shortly after he entered the cave and his books became covered in mildew so he was unable to read them.

By now, NASA had become interested in Siffre's experiments as part of their research into long-term space flight. They had supplied the expedition with the same food they would use on the *Apollo* missions, and were monitoring the experiment through a cable that was relaying biometric data from Siffre to the research team. Unfortunately, this cable would add to his discomfort by administering painful electric shocks when there were lightning storms around the cave.

This total isolation caused Siffre to become suicidal, his mental state declined, and aptitude tests he undertook showed that his manual dexterity and memory function reduced over the time he spent in the cave. Some effects would be long-lasting: he suffered from poor eyesight, memory loss and depression. Eventually, he divorced and reportedly fled to a South American rainforest, perhaps in an attempt to return to isolation.

NASA was now at the forefront of research into isolation as new frontiers in space opened up and deep space flight became a possibility. The *Apollo* crews who had landed on the Moon all experienced profound psychological effects caused by the isolation of space (similar to Siffre). Michael Collins, who commanded *Apollo 11* on the first Moon landing, became known as the 'loneliest man in history' as (alone) he passed behind the Moon some 384,000 km (238,600 miles) from Earth just as Neil Armstrong stepped on to the Moon for the first time.

After returning to Earth, the *Apollo* astronauts responded differently to the psychological pressure of their experience. Neil Armstrong became reclusive while Buzz Aldrin became mired in alcoholism and depression. Many marriages in the *Apollo* programme broke down. Perhaps the most extreme case was Edgar Mitchell, who experienced an 'intelligence' in space that he described as a 'flash of understanding' in which he became switched on to the universe. He would spend the rest of his life trying to understand his experience. Clearly, NASA had a problem for future space missions.

During preparations for a return to the Moon and sending people to Mars there have been several experiments to replicate the psychological isolation of deep space missions. One of the most recent was the Mars 500 Project, led by the Institute of Biomedical Problems of the Russian Academy of Sciences in 2010–11.

During the study, six participants from several countries spent 520 days in an enclosed module in Russia. Mild to moderate symptoms of depression were reported by one crew member throughout his time in confinement. Two others experienced disrupted sleep-wake cycles, while another experienced insomnia and physical exhaustion. The two most stressed and exhausted crew members were involved in 85 per cent of the perceived conflicts with the other crew members and mission control. Similar to the McGill studies of the 1950s, they also observed that the crew members became increasingly sedentary when awake and spent more time sleeping and resting.

COPING WITH ISOLATION

What can we learn from these studies about coping with isolation? The importance of routine and maintaining sleep-wake cycles (circadian rhythms) are essential for our mental well-being in isolation. Those who cope well with isolation set up routines early and stick to them. We have seen that a desire to stimulate our senses through food, entertainment and in some cases drugs to replace the stimulation we receive through social contact is a recurring theme. Quite simply, we become bored and our minds need occupying. Poor coping strategies such as overeating can be damaging to our physical health, and long-term loneliness can affect life expectancy. Those who fare well in isolation find other ways to stimulate their senses, through activities such as reading or listening to and creating music.

New technologies have certainly helped us to cope with modern stints of isolation. These include access to the internet, video streaming services to entertain us, and the ability to make reliable video calls to friends and family, allowing us to maintain social contact.

We have also learned that many of the psychological effects of isolation are short-lived. Research by Netta Weinstein and Thuy-vy Nguyen for the Royal Society looked at approximately 800 isolated adults in the USA and the UK. They measured their loneliness, depression and anxiety in the early weeks of the Covid-19 crisis and again measured mental health at two separate points after the lockdown. They were surprised to see that their loneliness, depression and anxiety did not increase under self-isolation. Some personality types may also have thrived during the lockdown, taking advantage of new opportunities to explore their creativity or enjoy the outdoors in seclusion.

43
Sleep

Sleep is a vital part of our daily routine. A typical adult requires around eight hours of sleep per night, and children up to 13 hours. Getting enough quality sleep at the right time is as essential as eating, drinking and exercising properly in order to maintain your health. Without sleep, you cannot create or maintain the neural connections in your brain that allow you to learn and form memories, affecting concentration and reaction times. The fact that we need sleep is indisputable, but the purpose of sleep is very much a matter for continued debate.

CIRCADIAN RHYTHMS

Sleep is controlled by your 'body clock', a biological rhythm evolved over millions of years. These circadian rhythms are dictated by the cycle of day and night over a 24-hour period. The internal body clock is present in all of our cells but is regulated by a circadian pacemaker in the hypothalamus called the suprachiasmatic nuclei (SCN). This is a cluster of thousands of cells that receive information about environmental light levels from the eyes. This acts to reset the circadian pacemaker so that the cycle of sleep is synchronized with the external environment.

The SCN controls the production of melatonin, a hormone that makes you sleepy. When light levels are reduced, the SCN tells the brain to make more melatonin, which encourages feelings of sleep. When it becomes light again, melatonin levels drop and you wake for the day. At the same time, there is a homeostatic control during the daytime, which alerts the body to declining energy levels, normally towards the end of the day, and you become tired in the evening and fall asleep.

The circadian rhythm has peaks and troughs throughout its cycle, with our strongest sleep drive typically occurring during two dips

Circadian rhythm

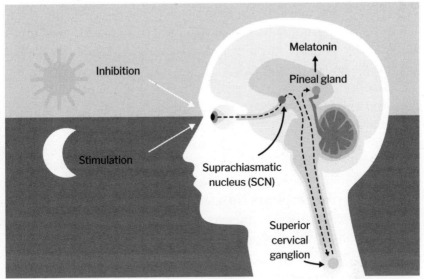

Our sleep cycles are linked to our circadian rhythm, which is governed by the transition of light between day and night.

between 2 am and 4 am and 1 pm and 3 pm (the lunchtime dip). The intensity of sleep we experience can also vary depending on how sleep-deprived we are.

TYPES OF SLEEP

Traditionally, sleep can be categorized as two different types: 1) rapid eye movement (REM) sleep and 2) non-REM sleep (which has three different stages). These are connected to specific brain waves and neural activity.

William C. Dement (1928–2020) was one of the first psychologists to describe REM sleep and its relationship with dreaming. In 1957, along with Nathaniel Kleitman (1895–1999), he discussed the specific sleep stages that together establish the night-time sleeping pattern of humans:

- Stage 1 non-REM sleep is the transition from wakefulness to sleep.
- Stage 2 non-REM sleep is a period of light sleep before you enter deeper sleep.
- Stage 3 non-REM sleep is the period of deep sleep that you need to feel refreshed in the morning.

REM sleep first occurs about 90 minutes after falling asleep. Your eyes move rapidly from side to side behind closed eyelids. Most of your dreaming occurs during REM sleep and your body becomes paralyzed to prevent injury and stop you acting out your dreams. As you sleep, you cycle through all stages of non-REM and REM sleep several times during a typical night, with prolonged and deeper REM periods occurring towards the end of the sleep cycle.

The internal circadian rhythm that governs sleep maintains a regular sleep-wake cycle even without external cues such as light. Cave explorer Michel Siffre subjected himself to extended periods of time living in underground cave systems. In order to study his circadian rhythms, he removed all external clues, such as clocks and access to daylight, and had no radio for communication. The only thing influencing when he woke, ate and then slept was his internal body clock.

After his first underground stay of 61 days in 1962, he resurfaced on 17 September believing the date was 20 August! This difference suggested that his natural rhythm had changed due to the lack of external cues, making him believe one day was longer than it was, and leading to him thinking that fewer days had passed. In later studies, when he was in his 60s, Siffre determined that his circadian rhythm beat to a slower pace than it had when he was a young man, sometimes stretching to 48 hours.

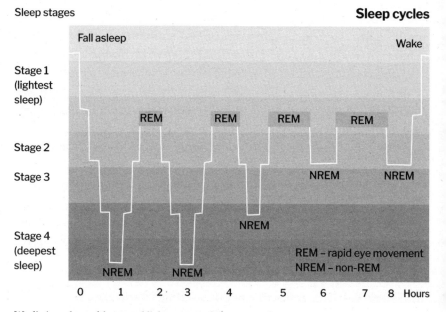

We dip in and out of deeper and lighter stages of sleep on a cycle.

Although the circadian rhythm can deviate from the standard 24-hour cycle, it resists any major adjustments in sleep pattern. If major disturbances did occur, the biological clock would become completely out of balance. People who experience jet lag will be acutely aware of the effects of this imbalance and it may take them days or weeks to recover.

THE IMPORTANCE OF SLEEP

The consequences of poor sleep have been known for more than a century. One of the first studies into sleep deprivation took place in Iowa University in 1896. Three volunteers were kept awake for up to 90 hours in the psychological laboratories at the university. Their reactions grew slower, memory declined and they struggled to retain focus as they became increasingly more sleep-deprived. One individual experienced visual hallucinations, imagining the air was full of coloured particles.

As well as adverse psychological impacts, the study revealed that the test subjects had also experienced physiological effects. There was reduced muscle function and a decline in body temperature. Fortunately, the effects were reversed after one good night's sleep and there was no long-term damage to the participants from the study.

More than a century of research has shown that long term the effects of poor sleep or a chronic lack of sleep lead to reduced mood, low resilience and poor interpersonal skills. As in the study, there are also physiological effects with an increase in the risk of disorders including high blood pressure, cardiovascular disease, diabetes, depression and obesity.

There are particular groups that are vulnerable to poor or chronic lack of sleep. A wide range of research shows that shift workers sleep less well than people who work typical daytime hours. One study found the greatest impact is on those working night shifts, whereby on average night shift employees sleep for 36 minutes less than daytime workers. Consequently, this group are more prone to the adverse psychological and physiological effects of poor sleep.

In 1960, William C. Dement (1928–2020) recognized the public health benefits of acknowledging and treating sleeping disorders. Sleep disorders are defined as a group of conditions that affect the ability to sleep well on a regular basis. They include conditions such as:

- **Insomnia:** The inability to fall asleep or to remain asleep.
- **Sleep apnea:** Pauses in breathing during sleep.

- **Parasomnias:** Disorders that cause abnormal movements and behaviours during sleep.
- **Narcolepsy:** Suddenly feeling extremely tired and falling asleep without warning.

STANFORD NARCOLEPTIC DOG COLONY

In 1970, Dement opened the Stanford Sleep Disorders Clinic. One area of research was tackling narcolepsy and people falling asleep at the wheel when driving a car. It was known that narcolepsy was hereditary and occurred disproportionately in the Dobermann breed of dog. Dement set up a narcoleptic dog colony at Stanford consisting of various breeds (all of which made useless guard dogs). They found that breeding some narcoleptic dogs did not produce narcoleptic offspring, whereas others, such as Dobermanns and Labradors, did pass on this trait genetically. This provided compelling evidence that there could be a genetic cause of narcolepsy.

However, breeding narcoleptic dogs was in itself a challenge. Researcher Lewanne Sharp recalls that 'When the male would get excited and mount the female, invariably he would fall asleep.' The colony ran from 1976 to 1995, and helped establish the cause of narcolepsy in humans. This was a leap forward in recognizing and treating sleep disorders. It also raised the question as to whether sleep and dreaming was a uniquely human experience.

Research using Dobermanns helped to reveal that there may be a genetic cause of the sleep disorder narcolepsy.

As mentioned, sleep is essential for recovery, memory storage and growth, so logically other animals need sleep, too. It appears that insects may undergo periods of inactivity but they have not been shown to sleep or enter an REM state. Siegel in 2008 found that some animals such as fish and amphibians reduce their neural activity but do not enter a state that we would define as sleep. However, REM sleep patterns have now been found in dragon lizards and cephalopods, broadening the influence of Bill Dement's research to more than 500 million years of animal evolution. This has important implications for why the deep sleep patterns we see in humans evolved and what function deep sleep performs in the human brain.

44
Personality

The exploration of temperament can be traced back to the theories of the philosophers and physicians of ancient Greece. They understood the cosmos to consist of four elements – water, fire, earth and air – and that these were the foundation of our bodies and therefore our temperament.

In fact, the terms that Hippocrates developed in 400 BCE are still applied to describing personality today: calm people were thought to have a higher level of phlegm and were described as 'phlegmatic'; optimistic people were believed to have more blood and were described as 'sanguine'; depressed people had a higher concentration of black bile and were referred to as 'melancholic'; and irritable people had more yellow bile and were thought of as 'choleric'. Hippocrates summarized that different personality types were caused by the balance of these bodily fluids.

Hippocrates' view that personality has a biological underpinning has resonated with modern theorists, who connect mood and behaviour with chemicals (neurotransmitters) in the brain, such as noradrenaline and serotonin. However, personality goes far beyond describing mood and temperament. Sigmund Freud's psychoanalytic approach is one of the most well-known theories that attempts to understand the mind and personality.

PSYCHODYNAMIC EXPLANATIONS FOR PERSONALITY
A fundamental assumption of the psychoanalytic approach is that unconscious motivations and needs play a role in determining our behaviour. Freud developed several hypothetical models of the mind and explored the concept of unconscious drives to help explain causes of behaviour, and therefore development of personality.

As outlined in more detail in Chapter 5, Freud explored how

personality developed through different stages and recognized how events in early childhood could affect behaviour and personality in later life. Gradually, psychologists would move away from Freudian principles to a more humanistic approach, which viewed individual experience as being more important, rather than people being victims of their unconscious motivations.

PERSONALITY AND PHYSIOLOGY

Similar to the ancient Greek philosophers, many of the early personality theorists considered personality to exist as different 'types', and be deep-rooted and hard to change. In 1954, William Sheldon (1898–1977), for example, grouped people according to three body types and connected these physical differences to variations in personality:

1. **Endomorphic** (described as fat and soft): Tend to be sociable and relaxed.
2. **Ectomorphic** (described as thin and fragile): Tend to be introverted and restrained.
3. **Mesomorphic** (described as muscular and hard): Tend to be aggressive and adventurous. They are callous and ruthless in relationships with others.

Sheldon found evidence for his theory by studying a cohort of 400 male college students. He found students that fit three categories: 1) non-delinquent students, 2) delinquent students and 3) criminal delinquent students. Sheldon collected photos of these students and rated them as having either an endomorphic, ectomorphic or mesomorphic body type. He found that the higher the delinquency, the higher the average mesomorphy rating.

However compelling Sheldon's results are, they must be viewed with caution. Sheldon studied only male students, meaning that his

Somatotype	Students	Delinquents	Criminal delinquents
Endomorph	3.2	3.5	3.4
Ectomorph	3.4	2.7	1.8
Mesomorph	3.8	4.6	5.4

Results from Sheldon's study of delinquent and non-delinquent college students.

findings cannot be generalized to the female population. Our view of what is considered 'delinquent' changes over time and between cultures and situations, so may not be a good measure of personality. Finally, research such as this doesn't demonstrate cause and effect. It could be the case that people born with a naturally mesomorphic body type are treated differently, possibly stigmatized, and that this was the cause of their delinquent behaviour.

Personality is far too complex to relate simply to body type and a more interactionist view is now common, accepting that multiple factors undoubtedly contribute to differences in personality.

PERSONALITY FACTORS

Modern theorists view personality traits as a continuous spectrum, rather than individual characteristics underlying behaviour. It's assumed that we all possess certain traits to a greater or lesser extent. By placing people on a trait continuum, psychologists can assess how high or low each individual is on any particular trait and make comparisons between people.

Hans Eysenck developed one of the best-known theories of personality, which has become both influential and controversial. Born in Berlin, Eysenck moved in 1934 to London, where he founded the Department of Psychology at the Institute of Psychiatry. He remains a controversial figure in psychology due to his involvement with research on the relationship between race and IQ. However, his research into personality offered an alternative to psychodynamic approaches and provided a foundation for modern cognitive behaviour therapy.

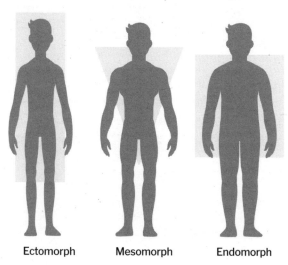

Ectomorph   Mesomorph   Endomorph

Sheldon (1954) argued that body type, or somatotype, was linked to personality: endomorphic body types have a tendency to be relaxed and outgoing; mesomorphic physiques are usually energetic and assertive; ectomorphic body types are fearful and restrained. Modern psychology has moved away from the idea that psychology can be mapped to body type.

It was while at the Maudsley Hospital in London during World War II that Eysenck began researching personality, working with 700 soldiers who were casualties of the war. Like theorists before him, Eysenck designed a questionnaire to measure personality traits. The first was the Personality Inventory, developed in 1969. This was then refined to become the Eysenck Personality Questionnaire, or EPQ, in 1975.

Eysenck argued that personality could be measured on a continuum of two traits: extraversion and neuroticism. People who complete his questionnaire and gain a high extraversion score are defined as outgoing and sociable, they may be risk-takers and are generally quite active. People with a high neuroticism score would be less sociable and more prone to becoming overwhelmed.

Eysenck added a biological element to his theory by linking personality with the action of the nervous system. He argued that people who are highly extraverted have an underaroused nervous system, and therefore require external stimulation and excitement to feel any sort of emotional arousal. Conversely, individuals who are highly introverted have a naturally overaroused or easily aroused nervous system, so need very little stimulation and will avoid exciting or stressful situations.

Later, Eysenck added psychoticism as another dimension to his model. He related this trait to elevated levels of testosterone. Those

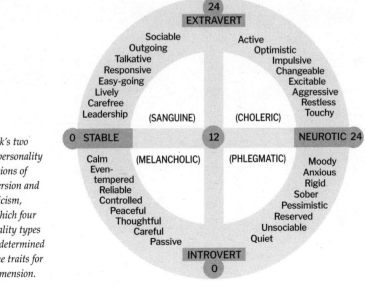

Eysenck's two major personality dimensions of extraversion and neuroticism, from which four personality types can be determined from the traits for each dimension.

scoring highly on psychoticism were described as egocentric, aggressive, lacking in empathy and impulsive. See also Chapter 48.

Some evidence has been found to support Eysenck's theories, for example Eysenck's own findings that a sample of 2,422 male prisoners recorded higher average scores of all three personality traits than those in a control group. This suggests that extremes of personality type may be a factor in offending behaviour. However, as with all research of this nature it is impossible to definitely state whether these ingrained personality factors caused the subsequent behaviour, or whether the behaviour itself and resulting consequences influenced the participants' responses to Eysenck's questionnaire.

45
Fear

Fear is an unpleasant emotion, but it helps us to respond to danger by focusing attention and increasing our ability to cope with the threat. The onset of the fear response can be rapid but declines once the threat has passed. The areas of the brain found to be linked to fear are also linked to learning and memory, which is not surprising when we consider that we probably do not wish to experience a fearful event more than once.

We have to remember how to avoid it. However, there are some people who do not respond to fear in ways that we would expect, and in fact appear to actively seek out fear-inducing situations time and time again.

'I must not fear. Fear is the mind-killer. Fear is the little-death that brings total obliteration. I will face my fear. I will permit it to pass over me and through me. And when it has gone past I will turn the inner eye to see its path. Where the fear has gone there will be nothing. Only I will remain.'
Frank Herbert (*Dune*)

UNUSUAL RESPONSES TO FEAR

In the early hours of Saturday 3 June 2017, Alex Honnold woke up in his van, put on his favourite red T-shirt, grabbed his climbing shoes and chalk bag and walked up to the base of the 914 m (3,000 ft) cliff of El Capitan in California. With no equipment except his hands and his climbing shoes, he began to climb up the imposing granite wall.

Upon completion of the first ascent of El Capitan in 1958, when asked why he climbed mountains, Warren Harding replied, 'Because we're insane!' This first ascent was so extreme it had taken almost a

Alex Honnold during a solo ascent of 'The Nose' on El Capitan (left) in Yosemite National Park, California. In most people, their fear response would prevent them from attempting such a feat.

year-and-a-half and used mechanical methods to scale the cliff. Now, Alex Honnold was undertaking something that was far beyond insane. With no protection, if he made one small mistake he would die. It's hard to imagine this undertaking. Even looking at a cliff face this large causes a fear response in most people. When a climber is on the rock face they report their fingertips sweating and pulsing with shocks of fear. Their heart is pounding. The position they are in is so paralyzing that they freeze. The documentary crew were so terrified during the filming of Honnold's ascent they had to use remote technologies to distance themselves from what they were witnessing. Yet, after three hours and 56 minutes, Alex Honnold pulled himself over the top of the rock face to achieve the impossible and free-solo El Capitan.

What allowed Alex Honnold to place himself in such an extreme position and not be consumed with fear?

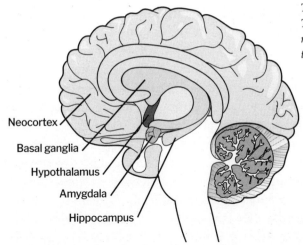

The anatomy of fear.
The amygdala is key to
regulating and controlling
the fear response.

Neocortex

Basal ganglia

Hypothalamus

Amygdala

Hippocampus

There are three parts to the fear response. The first is the fight-or-flight response, whereby physical arousal occurs in response to the threat. Physiological responses to fear include elevated heart rate, clammy hands, tense muscles and rapid breathing. This response evolved as a survival mechanism, allowing animals and humans to rapidly respond to life-threatening situations by fighting off the threat or fleeing to safety.

The second aspect is the cognitive response. This is when the individual evaluates the situation and considers the possible outcomes. The third and final aspect is the behavioural response, when an individual takes action to avoid or escape the threat.

The mechanism for responding to threat begins in an area of the brain called the amygdala. This is activated and combines sensory inputs (sight, sound, smell), with emotions linked to the fight-or-flight response, such as fear or anger. A distress signal is sent to the hypothalamus by the amygdala, which communicates with the rest of the body through the sympathetic nervous system. The amygdala then acts as a control centre to co-ordinate the fear response.

As discussed in Chapter 41, the body's response to threat utilizes two major systems. The first responds to sudden (acute) stressors such as personal attack. The sympathetic nervous system (SNS) transmits a signal, causing the hormone adrenaline to be released into the bloodstream. As adrenaline circulates through the body, it brings about a number of physiological responses. The heartbeat increases, leading to elevated blood pressure supplying more blood to the muscles, heart and other vital organs. In order to take up the maximum amount of oxygen, the breathing rate increases. The bloodstream is also saturated with glucose and fats to supply energy required for the fight-or-flight response.

When the stressor is no longer present, the threat response is dampened down by the autonomic nervous system (ANS). The parasympathetic part of the ANS slows the heartbeat and reduces blood pressure. It also restores digestion, which is shut off during the fear response, and the individual returns to a normal steady state of arousal.

The second system deals with longer-term ongoing (chronic) stressors such as a stressful work situation. If the brain continues to perceive something as threatening, the hypothalamus activates a stress response system, releasing a hormonal signal into the bloodstream to maintain the fear response from the SNS. Various stress-related hormones, such as cortisol, are then released by the adrenal glands. Cortisol is responsible for several effects in the body that are important in the fight-or-flight

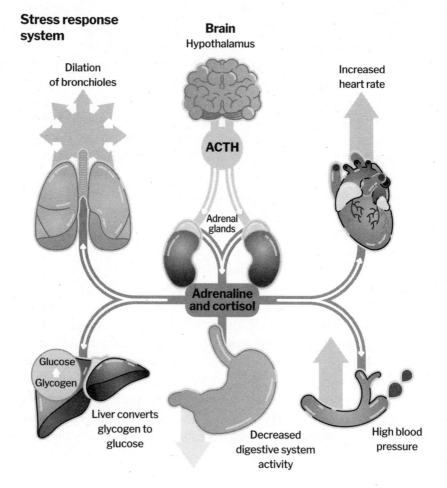

Stress response system

Brain
Hypothalamus

Dilation of bronchioles

Increased heart rate

ACTH

Adrenal glands

Adrenaline and cortisol

Glucose

Glycogen

Liver converts glycogen to glucose

Decreased digestive system activity

High blood pressure

response. This brings advantages such as rapid bursts of energy and decreased pain sensitivity. However, there are also drawbacks, including reduced cognitive performance and lowered immune response. If the stress response is prolonged, it can lead to long-term health conditions associated with stress.

The system also has an effective feedback mechanism. Special receptors in the hypothalamus and pituitary gland monitor cortisol levels in the body. If these rise above normal, they reduce the level of hormones activating the adrenal gland and restore cortisol levels back to normal.

BEHAVIOURAL EXPLANATIONS FOR FEAR

How we deal with danger can also be trained or conditioned. In Chapter 11, we explored the historical experiment by Watson and Rayner in 1920 that ushered in a century of research into fear conditioning. In the experiment, Little Albert was made to fear a rat by associating it with a loud, alarming sound. The experimental model of fear conditioning was further developed from the work of Ivan Pavlov (1927), who initially looked at appetitive conditioning processes in dogs to develop a general model for conditioning behaviour.

Little is known about the process of how fear response develops in early childhood. Evidence from a longitudinal study conducted by Gao et al. (2010) showed that fear conditioning increases as children get older but particularly so around five to six years old. This implies that our experiences in childhood could be crucial in conditioning our fear response. Central to this is the development of the amygdala, a small, almond-shaped clump of nuclei, deep in the temporal lobe, that acts as the locus of fear learning.

FEAR AND THE AMYGDALA

Recent research has shown that electrical stimulation of the amygdala in a calm animal can cause it to react in a fearful and/or aggressive way. Furthermore, studies have investigated shocking the feet of rats with an electrical current and associating this input with a flash of light. Rats that had their amygdala destroyed triggered a fear response to the foot shock, but did not learn to associate the fear response between the light and the foot shock. Despite several training sessions, the animals did not display any fear of the light alone. Looking past the dubious ethics of these studies, they give us compelling evidence of the link between the amygdala, fear and learning.

Humans with amygdala damage appear to display similar characteristics. Elizabeth Phelps and Joe LeDoux (2005) investigated mild fear conditioning in people with localized damage to the amygdala. They discovered that their subjects could associate the connection between the light and the shock by saying 'a light comes on, followed by a shock'. However, they did not display a typical fear response such as increased heart rate when they were shown only the light. LeDoux has also demonstrated changes in the patterns of communication between neurons in the amygdala, resulting from long-term fear conditioning in rats. Together, these results indicate that the amygdala is a key structure for fear learning.

In the film *Free Solo*, Alex Honnold undergoes an MRI scan on his brain. MRI is a type of scan that uses radio waves and powerful magnetic fields to produce detailed images of the inside of the body. It tested his response to fear stimuli and showed that he had very little activation in his amygdala. His amygdala was working, but required a large amount of stimulus to activate it.

The question remains whether the reduced activity in the amygdala has caused Honnold's lack of a fear response, or whether overstimulation of the amygdala in his youth has resulted in it requiring more stimulation as an adult to induce a fear response.

Amygdala
Fear centre of the brain

Alex Honnold's amygdala compared to that of a control subject.

This reduced activity in his amygdala is what allows Alex Honnold to manage the first stage of his fear response and avoid an immediate fight-or-flight reaction to the danger that is present when climbing a 914 m (3,000 ft) cliff face. Drawing on experience, he is able to weigh up the possible outcomes of his situation and make a calculated judgement about the risk he is facing. Through repeated training and rehearsal he is then able to focus, take action and make the necessary moves that allowed him to successfully free-solo El Capitan.

It may seem ridiculous to most of us that he would decide to override his fear response in this way, yet most of us undergo the same process when we drive a car. If we fail to turn the wheel at the correct time the consequences will be severe. We have conditioned our fear response in the same way and this allows us to drive the car safely to our destination. Extremists like Alex Honnold will have to engage in what gamblers term 'deep play', whereby you have bet everything against an uncertain outcome in order to elicit the fear response. In this way, the games climbers play becomes an addictive elixir, chasing their fear and pushing the limits ever further.

46

Aggression

Part of the difficulty in researching aggression and the causes of violent behaviour is how to define aggression in the first place. Typically, animals tend to display patterns of violence for obvious reasons, such as fighting to gain food or territory. Classifying aggression becomes more difficult with humans and non-human primates because of the complexity of both our intentions and group dynamics.

Aggression can be predatory in order to gain resources, social in order to establish dominance or a new place in a hierarchy, or defensive in order to protect the individual. In this chapter, we will discuss the biological and behavioural theories behind aggression.

AGGRESSION AND THE BRAIN

In Chapter 45, we learned how the limbic system, principally the hypothalamus and the amygdala, control the fear in response to a perceived threat. A large body of evidence also suggests that as well as regulating fear response, the amygdala has a key function in mediating aggression and violence.

Evidence for the link between aggression and the amygdala comes from animal studies by Heinrich Klüver (1897–1979) and Paul Bucy (1904–92) in 1939. They studied monkeys that had had their temporal lobes removed, resulting in the animals showing little fear, and becoming incredibly docile. Later research into what was then called Klüver-Bucy syndrome showed that this was likely due to the interference that had taken place with the amygdala of the monkeys, as selective removal of that part of the brain produced similar effects on fear and aggression.

Similarly, human aggression can also be affected by damage to the amygdala. Charles Whitman, who carried out a sniper attack from

the University Tower at Texas in 1966, left a note in which he outlined how he had sought help for his violent impulses leading up to the attack. Whitman's autopsy showed that he had a tumour pressing on his amygdala that could have led to his apparent change in behaviour, which resulted in him killing 16 people.

There are also people who have underlying conditions in which the amygdala is not necessarily damaged, but does not operate in a typical manner, such as in a psychiatric disorder called intermittent explosive disorder (IED). People who have the condition are prone to sudden bursts of aggression. They have also been shown to perform poorly on facial emotion recognition tasks. Studies using facial recognition of emotions while undergoing brain scans found that the amygdalas of IED participants were more active than those of volunteers when looking at images of faces expressing anger. This difference in reaction to angry faces could be one explanation for the extreme and sudden aggression shown by IED patients: their brains react differently to a perceived threat.

Perhaps one of the largest studies to date using neuroimaging techniques was by Adrian Raine and his colleagues in 1997. This used positron emission tomography (PET) scans to analyze brain activity in 41 people awaiting trial for murder, compared to activity in 41 control subjects. The study found that there was reduced activity in the prefrontal cortex as well as increased activity in the thalamus of people convicted of murder.

PET scans thus provided the best evidence yet that brain dysfunction could be linked to some types of aggression and violence. However, Raine emphasized that the study did not imply that differences in brain functioning caused aggressive behaviour, and that it was not possible to predict, using brain scans or otherwise, who may or may not go on to commit violent crimes.

GENETIC EVIDENCE FOR AGGRESSION

In 1993, psychologist Hans Brunner and his team studied a Dutch family with a history of violent behaviour. Several of its male members were known to be aggressive, and had a history of serious violent crime, including rape and arson. One of the men had even tried to run down his employer with a car when he was accused of substandard work.

There appeared to be a pattern to their behaviour, which could have a possible genetic link. Brunner found that all of the men in this family had a particular form of a gene that was responsible for regulating serotonin levels in the brain. The gene is responsible for the production of monoamine oxidase A (MAOA), an enzyme that works to break down serotonin and other neurotransmitters once they have been transmitted across a synapse. It could be that the low levels of MAOA caused serotonin levels to become unbalanced and contributed to the aggressive behaviour of the men. Studies in mice have shown that the neurotransmitter serotonin plays a key role in modulating aggressive and violent behaviour.

It is also important to note that the defective MAOA gene codes on the X chromosome and are passed on from the mother. Girls will inherit an X chromosome from both parents so the defective gene is effectively diluted. In males, however, the defect is passed on in full, making it more likely that men could develop an aggression disorder. This may be one reason why males are more aggressive and violent than females. However, we risk falling into a deterministic trap if we attempt to attribute all violent and aggressive behaviour to biological causes.

The use of modern brain scanning techniques has given us a window into the mind like never before. They indicate that in some cases, differences in the structure and function of the brain can cause heightened levels of aggression. However, as Adrian Raine commented, it is not possible to predict violent behaviour based on an individual's brain scan. Furthermore, the example of Jim Fallon's family history of psychopathy (see below) shows that even if an individual is genetically predisposed to aggressive behavioural traits, given the right environmental upbringing a person may never develop these behaviours.

BEHAVIOURAL EXPLANATIONS FOR AGGRESSION

There is evidence that environmental conditioning may play an important role in the emergence of aggressive behaviours. Social learning theory (SLT) proposes that we learn through observation of others. Therefore, we learn from the situations we experience how aggressive behaviour is enacted and the form it takes. As discussed in Chapter 29, the Bobo doll studies by Bandura et al. (1961) showed that where aggressive behaviour was observed by children, they were more likely to imitate aggressive behaviour themselves.

Jim Fallon (2005)

In 2005, neuroscientist James (Jim) Fallon (born 1947) was asked to carry out a study using PET scans of some of the most notorious serial killers in the USA in order to find patterns in the brain that may be linked to psychopathic tendencies.

Jim noticed that one of the scans was a good match for someone who fitted the profile of a psychopath. He looked up the code for the scan (the identity of the individual had been kept from him to ensure impartiality) and to his horror realized the PET scan was of his own brain. He was the pathological psychopath! Further discussion with

Jim Fallon   Lizzie Borden

his mother revealed that he comes from a long line of murderers and serial killers, including Lizzie Borden (1860–97), who was infamously accused of killing her father and stepmother in 1892. However, despite his genetic background, which included a variant of the MAOA gene linked with aggression, he is happily married, non-violent and has a successful academic career.

Fallon's research would later show that childhood trauma was essential to triggering aggression in later life. While some people may have a biological predisposition to violent or aggressive behaviour, it takes a trigger from the environment to cause that behaviour. This is known as the 'diathesis-stress model'.

One of the strongest arguments for aggression having a behavioural cause is the frustration–aggression theory, which emerged in the 1930s. Frustration occurs when an internal or external factor prevents us from achieving a goal. John Dollard (1900–80) and his colleagues proposed that the existence of frustration always led to some form of aggression. However, this definition supposes that aggression will always result from frustration. Yet we all get frustrated but not everyone becomes aggressive. In answer to this, frustration–aggression theory suggests that the intensity of the aggression is greatest when directed at the source of the frustration as a type of retaliatory behaviour.

Psychodynamic theory argues that this cathartic release of frustration was necessary to protect our ego. This could occur by using aggression appropriately in sports ('sublimation') or by outwardly deflecting our aggression on to something or someone else ('displacement'). Displacement occurs when it is impossible or improper to direct aggression at the source of the frustration. We see examples of this in our everyday life. For example: a driver who has been stuck in a traffic jam yelling at a cyclist; someone in the workplace who is frustrated with their computer and breaks the keyboard; or at home, throwing a leftover bag of screws across the room after trying to assemble flat-packed furniture for several hours. At some point in our lives it is therefore likely we have experienced aggression that has resulted from frustration.

Behavioural explanations can only go so far in explaining the causes of aggression. Nearly everyone will have felt frustrated, jealous or distrusting at some point in their lives yet we do not all resort to extremes of aggression and violence. Heightened aggression in individuals is likely to be a combination of genetics, biology and environmental conditioning. Some people will have a genetic predisposition to aggressive behaviour, but environmental conditioning plays an equally important role in triggering aggressive and violent behaviours in these individuals.

47
Deindividuation

The loss of individual rational thought and behaviour is a phenomenon first investigated in the classic crowd theory research of Gustave Le Bon in 1895. At the time, French society was violent and there were many protests. He looked at how an individual's impulsive behaviour was caused by being part of a group. Le Bon saw that the individual became anonymous in the crowd, and coupled with suggestibility and contagion this led to the 'collective mind' taking over the individual's decision-making.

This loss of self-control would allow them to go against their personal or social norms, resulting in the undesirable behaviour witnessed in the street riots of 19th-century France.

Throughout the 20th century, crowd theory was refined. The term 'deindividuation' was first used in the 1950s by the American social psychologist Leon Festinger (1919–89) to describe situations in which people cannot be individuated or isolated from others, and therefore become hidden in the group. It is characterized by a decreased concern with how others perceive the individual and judge their actions.

In some cases, this can lead to positive social behaviours ('prosocial') as seen at large music festivals and religious gatherings. Altered consciousness through the use of drugs and alcohol also serves to increase deindividuation at these events. Prosocial deindividuation can lead to increased altruistic acts, such as giving money to charity, which goes some way to explaining why events such as the 'Live Aid' concert in 1985 are such an effective model for raising money for charitable causes.

During normal social situations, many people will refrain from aggressive and unreasonable behaviour. However, being anonymous in a crowd effectively means that the individual is unaccountable. This

The 2011 London riots saw a large number of individuals behave in a deindividuated way as the initial cause of social unrest was largely forgotten and the focus turned to looting and violent protest.

has the effect of reducing the inner restraints the individual has on their behaviour, leading to diminished fear of negative evaluation by others and reduced guilt over their actions. They feel liberated to do what they like. Zimbardo argued that the crowd diminishes our awareness and individuality and the larger the crowd, the greater the effect.

One example of this negative group behaviour is the phenomenon of baiting. Mann (1981) looked at 21 suicide leaps in the USA that had been reported in the newspapers throughout the 1960s and 1970s. Out of these cases, there were ten in which a crowd had formed to watch the suicide attempt, and baiting occurred. The crowd had encouraged the person to jump! He found that most incidents occurred at night-time and where the 'jumper' was high above the crowd and thus distanced from the personal situation. These aspects meant the people in the crowd had become deindividuated and this led them to taunt the jumper and encourage them to leap to their death. The way we communicate through online and mobile technologies has exacerbated the phenomenon, whereby people engage in impulsive and antisocial behaviours and baiting occurs. Cyberbullying through online platforms and electronic devices can lead to drug and alcohol abuse, psychological disorders and, in some extreme cases, suicide.

One of the most tragic examples is the suicide of Tyler Clementi, an 18-year-old student studying at Rutgers University, USA. He had recently begun the journey of embracing his homosexuality and coming out to

Rutgers students pay tribute to Tyler Clementi.

his friends and family. Cyberbullying can affect anyone, but lesbian, gay, bisexual and transgender (LGBT) students are most likely to be the targets of online abuse.

Tyler asked his room-mates for some privacy one evening as he had a date. Unbeknown to Tyler, his room-mate Dharun Ravi secretly positioned his computer so that a remote webcam was filming the room. The footage of the sexual encounter that occurred between Tyler and his male friend was then broadcast by Ravi and shared across the internet by other students. Rather than report the abuse, students were acting in a deindividuated way as they were able to remain anonymous, allowing them to participate in the humiliation and ridicule the online crowd had engaged in. On 22 September 2010, Tyler updated his Facebook status: 'Jumping off the gw bridge sorry'.

In this case, the anonymity afforded by the internet led to tragic consequences for the victim. For many, though, this anonymity can result in desirable behaviours and lead to positive outcomes. Adolescents report that they feel more comfortable seeking support for mental health issues rather than reporting these in person. This undoubtedly has led to improved outcomes and support for an area of health that has historically been overlooked and under-reported.

On the flip side, cultural differences and deindividuation can be a deadly cocktail. Robert Watson (1973) researched how warriors in 23 societies changed their appearance prior to violent conflict with neighbouring tribes. He found that there was a greater level of violence inflicted on the victims by societies whose warriors had become deindividuated through war paint and tribal costumes. As Zimbardo (2007) comments, when we want '... usually peaceful young men to harm and kill other young men ... it is easier to do so if they first change their appearance to alter their usual external facade'. In this sense, again the internet feeds into our ability to change our external facade and promote extremist views.

To investigate this, Awan et al. (2019) analyzed more than 100,000 tweets and 100,000 YouTube comments. They found that the design of social media networks can create echo chamber environments in which users are afforded high levels of anonymity, allowing for the dissemination of extremist views. The process of radicalization is extremely complex but one aspect is the individual being able to have extreme views and to have these views validated and reinforced. Social media platforms create a space for like-minded individuals to cluster together, where they are protected from alternative perspectives, which in turn reinforces the group's beliefs. In this way, we can see sections of the online community become cyber mobs, and extremist groups are able to radicalize vulnerable members of society.

Perhaps the most extreme case is the rise of Pepe the Frog. Pepe was created by artist and illustrator Matt Furie and first appeared in 2005 in the comic *Boy's Life*. He began life as a carefree pot-smoking frog who liked pizza and had the catchphrase 'feels good man'. By 2009, images of Pepe were still freely circulating the internet but had become more sinister, with Pepe depicted wearing Nazi uniforms with the 'feels good' catchphrase. The Anti-Defamation League thus listed Pepe as an official hate symbol.

The rise of Pepe was accompanied by the increased popularity of internet chat rooms such as 4Chan, which allowed users to post whatever they liked in complete anonymity. In this way, users could promote extreme right-wing ideology without fear of evaluation or negative judgement. Indeed, they instead received positive reinforcement from the group. By now, Matt Furie had completely lost control of his creation but what was to happen next was even more incredible.

In the 2016 US election, Hillary Clinton referred to Donald Trump and his supporters (the alt right) as a 'basket of deplorables'. Within a couple of weeks, Donald Trump's son had posted a photo of him in a line-up with Pepe titled 'The Deplorables' in a play on the film *The Expendables*. Trump's campaign thus leveraged the sentiment and language from the chat rooms before they were forced to disassociate from the character due to the controversy of anti-Semitism and racist ideology the symbol of Pepe now represented. Pepe in effect served as a facade or symbol for the alt right to unite behind. As in the studies by Watson looking at how warriors in tribes changed their image, using the image of Pepe allowed internet trolls to direct far more aggression and violence towards their victims than they would have done as an individual.

The echo chambers of the social media platforms allow for people to act in a deindividuated way but have a global reach. Deindividuation and how internet companies manage online anonymity therefore has a hugely important role to play in the future of modern society.

48
Criminal Psychology

Crime takes on many forms, from individual aggressive acts to large-scale corporate crime, making it an incredibly fascinating area of research but difficult to underpin with one overarching theory. In this chapter, we will instead look at an overview of big developments in the study of the criminal mind and gain a greater insight into how far we have come since the early days of criminal psychology.

LOMBROSO AND THE ATAVISTIC FEATURES OF CRIMINALS

At the end of the 19th century, the Italian physician Cesare Lombroso (1835–1909) founded the Italian School of Criminology, and became one of the pioneers of the scientific study of criminal behaviour. Lombroso believed that criminals were individuals who had failed to evolve at the same pace as the remainder of the human race, and that they could be identified by their physical characteristics, which indicated their biological inferiority. He called these 'atavistic' features, meaning 'ancient' or 'ancestral'. Lombroso further suggested that specific types of criminal had specific features, for example he proposed that murderers have bloodshot eyes and a hooked nose, whereas sex offenders have thick lips and protruding ears.

Lombroso based his ideas on data gathered from autopsies on convicted criminals, finding that 40 per cent of those he studied did indeed have the features. However, without a control group to compare these findings to it may simply have been that 40 per cent of the entire population possessed these features. Furthermore, any correlation between physical features and criminal behaviour would not imply a cause and effect relationship, and it could in fact be the case that having unusual facial features results in social stigmatization, which in turn forces people into crime.

TYPES DE CRIMINELS ITALIENS.

Portraits of Italian criminals from Cesare Lombroso's collection, 1895.

Lombroso's theories are now largely discredited. They are seen as incredibly socially sensitive, implying that some members of society are inherently genetically inferior and supporting discriminatory ideals with little reliable evidence. However, even flawed theories invite progress through their criticism, and Lombroso remains a key figure in the early study of criminology.

BIOLOGICAL CAUSES OF CRIMINAL BEHAVIOUR

The concept of a biological cause for criminality is still a popular one, especially when focusing on violent crime. The chapters on fear and aggression outline arguments for the amygdala being implicated in aggressive behaviour, and how specific genes, such as the MAOA gene, may also play a role. However, these biological theories often lead us towards what is known as a 'diathesis-stress argument' for aggressive behaviour and crime. That is, we may be genetically or biologically predisposed to a certain behaviour, but it requires stress from the environment to cause us to display that behaviour. In any case, the concept of an inherited cause for criminality is still a popular one, and one that we have not discussed so far is the XYY chromosome theory.

Around 1 in 1,000 newborn males has two Y chromosomes rather than one, and while this chromosome profile is relatively rare in the general population, it has been found to be common in the prison population. It has been found that XYY males tend to develop normally in most ways, but may have some learning issues such as distractibility and hyperactivity. These tendencies, combined with the demands of modern living, could be what cause a higher proportion of XYY males to find themselves in prison.

Further evidence of a possible genetic cause of criminal behaviour is suggested by psychologist Adrian Raine (whose PET scans of murderers is discussed in Chapter 46), who in 1993 performed a review of all the twin studies of criminal behaviour conducted up to that time. He found that these studies suggested that monozygotic (identical) twins were much more likely to have similar rates of criminal behaviour than dizygotic (non-identical) twins. Essentially, if one identical twin was a criminal, the other was more likely to also be a criminal. This suggests a genetic cause of criminality, although it is very difficult to separate the effects of genetics and environment.

It could be argued that identical twins are more likely to be treated in an identical way, therefore exaggerating the effect that the environment is having on the similarity in their behaviours. However, earlier research in 1984 by Sarnoff Mednick (1928–2015) et al. compared adopted criminals with their biological and adoptive fathers in Denmark. They measured the percentages of criminal convictions for the adoptees based on whether their biological or adoptive parents had criminal convictions, and found that there was a significant correlation between adoptees and their biological parents for convictions of property crimes, but not violent crimes. However, it is still difficult to disentangle possible environmental causes for these correlations. The adoptees had often spent the first few years of their lives with their biological parents and may still have had contact with them.

Hans Eysenck (discussed in more detail in Chapter 44) suggested that differences in our personalities are a fundamental cause of criminal behaviour, but that these differences are caused by both environmental and biological factors. Eysenck developed a questionnaire that could identify certain personality traits, such as extraversion, neuroticism and in later versions, psychoticism. He argued that these personality traits were influenced by our environment and also our biology. Eysenck suggested that a person who is extraverted and seeks thrills may do so because their nervous system is underaroused. It requires more stimulation to be activated, so they seek thrills in order to activate their nervous system and feel the excitement that others would experience with less extreme behaviour. This in turn may lead them to the thrill-seeking behaviour of crime.

Similarly, those people who score highly on neuroticism may have an overactive nervous system that responds very quickly to stimulus. This may cause them to overreact to stimulation from their environment, for example an argument or stressful situation, and therefore lash out in a violent way.

Critics argue that it is very difficult to provide evidence for Eysenck's theory, and in using his own questionnaire to prove his point he created a self-fulfilling prophecy.

SOCIAL INFLUENCE AND CRIMINAL BEHAVIOUR

The final area we will explore in relation to criminal behaviour is that of the role of society. Edwin Sutherland (1883–1950) in 1939 suggested that two factors are required for a person to become a criminal: 1) they need

	Convicted biological parents	Not convicted biological parents
Convicted adoptive parents	24.5%	14.7%
Not convicted adoptive parents	20.0%	13.5%

Percentage of adoptees with criminal convictions (Mednick et al., 1984).

to learn certain values that would support criminal behaviour, and 2) they need to learn the skills necessary to perform the crime. This theory is called differential association theory, and argues that criminals are primarily influenced by those they socialize with. This theory has some similarities with social learning theory, which is discussed in Chapter 29. In this chapter, we explained how Albert Bandura (1963) argued that our behaviour is learned during our lifetime through observation and imitation. In this way, criminals are not born, but are made through observation of those around them.

While only a few insights of key research are given here, we hope that it is clear that pinpointing one cause for the vast variety of crime would be both foolhardy and impossible. The causes of criminal behaviour are as complex as the variety of crimes. Research into the causes of criminal behaviour continues to be a vast and evolving field, but those theories that offer us possible solutions are those that are most useful to us.

Personality differences between prisoners and controls (Eysenck and Eysenck, 1977)

Hans and Sybil Eysenck assessed 2,070 male prisoners using the Eysenck Personality Questionnaire, which gives scores on psychoticism, extraversion and neuroticism, as well as including questions designed to detect lies. They compared these results to those of a control group of 2,422 men who did not have any criminal convictions.

They found that prisoners recorded higher scores than the control group on all personality measures, suggesting that criminality could be linked to extremes in personality type. However, they also found that these scores decreased with age in both groups.

Eysenck believed that extremes of each personality trait and interaction with the environment could lead to criminal behaviour:

• Extraverts seek more arousal, so will engage in dangerous activities.
• Neurotics will over-react to situations of threat.
• Psychotics are aggressive and lack empathy.

However, it can be argued that the prison environment or criminal lifestyle itself may encourage these extremes of personality, therefore negating any cause and effect relationship that may exist.

49

Psychology as a Science

Despite efforts since the earliest days of Wundt and his colleagues to establish psychology as an experimental, objective science, it is still often accused of not being a 'real' science. It is a legitimate argument that the very nature of studying an abstract concept, such as happiness, does not lend itself to the carefully controlled rigour of traditional science such as physics, in which variables can be carefully controlled and manipulated, and their outcomes measured precisely.

Dr Alex Berezow, executive editor of *Big Think* magazine and 'junk science' debunker, argues that psychology cannot be considered a science because it all too often does not meet the five basic requirements to be considered scientifically rigorous. Berezow states that a scientific discipline must have: 1) clearly defined terminology, 2) quantifiable measures, 3) highly controlled experimental conditions, 4) reproducibility and 5) predictability.

However, others argue that these requirements are too rigid, and that other disciplines that are considered scientific also do not meet them. Some also argue that not all of these requirements are in fact necessary in defining a science. For example, physicist David Deutsch argues that predictability, the idea that a good scientific theory can be used to make predictions about a future outcome, is not a good measure of a science. He argues that you may watch a magician perform a trick several times and therefore be able to predict what he will do, but that does not mean that you understand how it was done. Deutsch argues that it is the *understanding* that is more important.

However we decide to define what is and is not a science, many approaches in psychology can employ the scientific method as it is commonly understood to great effect. As a result, many argue that the myriad diverse studies in psychology should really be considered as being on a spectrum in terms of their use of the scientific method, rather than judging psychology as a whole on its credentials as a science.

REPEATABILITY AND OBJECTIVE MEASURES

One element of a scientific approach is to have studies that create results that are measurable and repeatable, so that they can be tested again and again for reliability. These results must be objective outcomes, free from any subjective bias from the researcher in question. When considering approaches such as the psychodynamic approach, we can see clearly that concepts such as psychosexual stages or unconscious desires are not measurable in any concrete way. They cannot be considered scientific, empirically testable ideas, and are laden with the subjective opinion of their creator. However, in the case of behavioural psychology, research does produce measurable data that can be, and indeed has been, repeated and shown to be reliable. For example, Skinner used very specific controlled conditions during his experiments on operant conditioning and both his procedures and results were carefully documented. Results such as these are free from subjective opinion and can be considered a truly objective application of the scientific method to studying behaviour.

FALSIFIABILITY

This concept of objective testing leads us to another criticism of psychology as a science, that of falsifiability. For a theory to be falsifiable it must be testable. One famous example to illustrate this point is Bertrand Russell's chocolate teapot analogy. Russell claimed that if he stated that a chocolate teapot orbited the Sun, and was too small to be seen by a telescope, he shouldn't expect people to believe him just because he could not be proven wrong. The burden of proof fell to him. However, as the claim was not measurable it could not be proven true or false, and was therefore not falsifiable. Russell was illustrating the point that we cannot assert that something might be true, just because we cannot prove that it is not true. This is the case again for the much-maligned field of psychodynamic psychology, where much of our behaviour is explained through unconscious, unobservable processes.

The scientific method

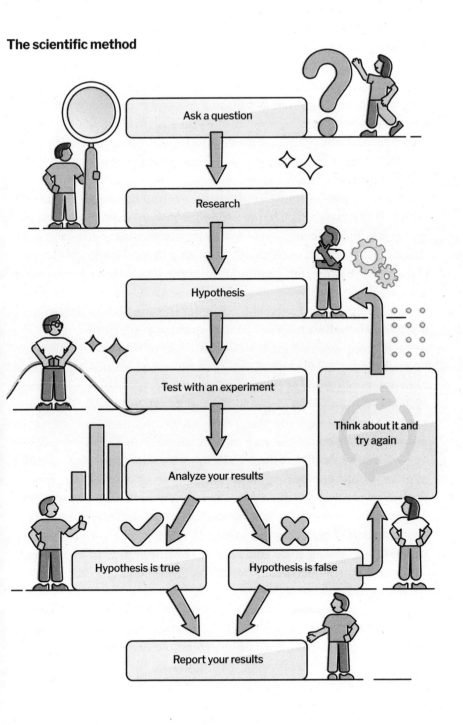

Ask a question

Research

Hypothesis

Test with an experiment

Analyze your results

Think about it and try again

Hypothesis is true

Hypothesis is false

Report your results

CONTROLS

Another issue in psychological research is finding control groups. In order to see if the variables you have manipulated in an experiment are what have affected the outcome, and not some other variable, you need a control group that is the same as your experimental group in every way apart from the one variable you wish to change and measure the effect of. With complex subjects like human beings, it is incredibly difficult to find two groups of people large enough to give valid results, and similar enough to compare.

For example, in Raine et al.'s study of the brains of murderers, which is discussed in Chapter 46, efforts were made to match the group of criminals being studied with a control group of non-criminals. Raine et al. matched each murderer with a control participant based on factors that they thought could influence their results, for example gender (there were two women and 39 men in each group), whether or not they suffered from schizophrenia (six murderers did, so they included six sufferers in his control group), and age (the mean age in each group was similar). However, even with these efforts being taken there are still many variables that Raine and his colleagues could not reasonably account for given that murderers willing to undergo PET scans for a piece of psychological research are probably very hard to come by. Each murderer may have committed their crime for a different reason: some may have resulted from sudden bursts of aggression while others may have been premeditated and planned attacks. Could comparing these brains give us a valid insight into the brains of all murderers? Also, how could we possibly know if the control group were not in fact themselves murderers who had just not been caught? It may seem an outlandish claim, but it highlights the difficulty of finding truly comparable control groups in psychology.

Even a psychological study such as Raine et al.'s, which bears all the hallmarks of rigorous science – objective measures using PET scans, control groups, repeatable procedures – still falls foul of scientific scrutiny when we delve more deeply into its procedures. In fact, due to the nature of the independent variable in this study (the criminal status of the participant) being an existing condition of the individual and not actually something that was manipulated by the experimenter, it is not considered an experiment at all but rather a quasi-experiment. As a result, causal conclusions cannot be justified. We cannot say from the results whether murderers have brains that inherently behave differently to the general population, or whether their brains have become different since committing their crime, maybe due to the event itself or the incarceration that followed.

In conclusion, there is no easy answer to the question of whether or not psychology should be considered a science. A more fruitful debate may be whether or not the study of psychology is useful to us, and what benefits it brings.

50

Controversies in Psychology

As you will have no doubt noticed throughout this book, psychological research encompasses many methods and its theories propose many different explanations for human behaviour. As a result, there are many criticisms to be considered when settling on what you think may be the best explanation for a given question in psychology.

Is the approach too deterministic, and is that a problem? Has a complex human behaviour been reduced down to a single explanation that is too simplistic? Can we really generalize findings to the whole human population if they have only been gathered from a few students in one university? In this chapter we will review some of the major areas of controversies in psychology and why they are important.

DETERMINISM AND FREE WILL

Determinism is the supposition that all events, including human behaviour, are predetermined by external factors. These factors may be biological or environmental, but they are out of the control of the individual and therefore a deterministic approach implies that humans have no free will or agency over their behaviour. This is of course a difficult concept for many people to accept, partly because it also implies that we cannot therefore be held accountable for our actions. Without free will, there can be no direct responsibility for our actions.

Many of the approaches we have discussed in this book would suggest that our behaviour is determined by outside factors, for example:

Reggie and Ronnie Kray were identical twins, from a violent criminal family, so they were potentially subject to a double dose of negative deterministic tendencies: genes and environment. Does this render them, and others like them, less accountable for their crimes?

- Psychodynamic approach: Behaviour is determined by our childhood experience and unconscious processes.
- Behavioural approach: Behaviour is learned through our responses to stimuli in our environment.
- Cognitive approach: Behaviour is determined by internal mental processes.
- Biological approach: Behaviour is determined by our physiology, hormones, neurotransmitters, genes and evolutionary pressures.

However unsettling this may seem, determinism is a necessary school of thought for psychology. In order to study a concept scientifically a researcher must isolate certain variables so that they can manipulate them and measure the effect this has on behaviour. This means that it is necessary for psychologists to assume that certain behaviours are caused by individual factors in order to study them. However, in reality of course, they would acknowledge the influence of many factors on our complex behaviour.

REDUCTIONISM AND HOLISM

Reductionism is a necessary process in science. It involves breaking down a complex subject into smaller, measureable parts. In this way, specific variables can be identified and manipulated by researchers, allowing them to change one small thing and measure the effect it has. To reduce psychological research to simple, measurable factors in this way was the original goal of Wundt and his colleagues when they attempted to separate experimental psychology from the more philosophical views that were popular at the time. However, in all science but especially in psychology, reducing a complex problem down to small parts can mean that you miss how the whole system affects the problem at hand.

In psychology for example, we may reduce the study of disorders such as depression down to the study of neurotransmitters. There is a belief that serotonin deficiency may play a role in depression, or that depression may be linked to a deficiency of many neurotransmitters. This knowledge then helps us to develop drugs such as selective serotonin reuptake inhibitors (SSRIs), which can be used to treat depression, and in this way a reductionist approach has enabled us to isolate a possible explanation for a behaviour and use a therapy linked to that explanation to enhance a person's well-being.

However, a reductionist approach such as this focusing only on biology would ignore other factors that may influence the experience of depression. An explanation from the cognitive approach, for example, may posit that faulty thinking was the cause and suggest cognitive behavioural theory as a solution. The psychodynamic approach, by contrast, may propose that the depression may be caused by an ego defence mechanism at work, such as repression, and that a solution would be to use free association or dream analysis to uncover the underlying trauma.

A holistic approach attempts to consider the impact of many different factors. Approaches in psychology such as Gestalt, humanism, positive and social psychology apply a holistic approach. Early examples of holism can be seen in the study of perception, in which psychologists argued that how we perceive sensory information biologically in the form of sounds or images only has meaning when it is combined with cognitive functions such as memory or emotion to place the input in some kind of understandable context. The letters that you are reading now only have meaning because you are using your memory to recall what each set of symbols mean, and putting them in the wider context of the book you know you are reading.

In the study of psychology, holistic approaches may consider how our biology interacts with our cognition, our experiences, and so influence our behaviour. This is useful in recognizing the wider context of behaviour and what influences it. However, theories that use this method of reasoning are difficult to provide empirical evidence for.

RESEARCH BIAS

Historically, much of psychological research has been conducted by Western industrialized cultures. Specifically, male members of Western industrialized cultures. This presents a problem when we consider that much of our behaviour is influenced by the customs, rules, morals and even language of the culture in which we reside. For example, studies such as Mary Ainsworth's 'strange situation' (discussed in Chapter 36) assume certain healthy behaviours in an infant that are based on the expectations of Western individualist society. A child who is not concerned about the whereabouts of their parent in this study may be considered to have a poor attachment to the parent; however, if this study were repeated in

Sigmund Freud and many of his peers and those who followed, were white, European males, giving them a particular bias when studying different aspects of psychology.

a society in which children are raised collectively, the ability of a child to interact with strange adults freely and without concern may be seen as normal and healthy.

The development of a theory in this way is known as an 'emic' approach, whereby the values of one culture are used to inform research and conclusions. Similarly, an imposed 'etic' is where we judge the behaviour of another culture based on our own values, for example judging a child from another culture to have a poor attachment style based on a Western value.

There are many similar examples included throughout this book. For example, the Social Readjustment Rating Scale developed by Holmes and Rahe is based on judgements of the stressful nature of events that may not translate to other cultures, and psychometric measures of intelligence assume certain perceptive skills that may not be accessible to some. Attempts to correct or acknowledge these issues can in themselves result in bias. 'Alpha bias' is a tendency to exaggerate differences between two groups, to assume that they are different based on some factor, whereas 'beta bias' is a tendency to diminish these differences.

These biases do not only exist between cultures, but also within them. The historical context of a theory is relevant when judging how applicable it is to modern behaviour. For example, Freud's theories of psychosexual development are subject to Victorian values in relation to the family and parenting. Mothers are assumed to be the primary caregiver, with other parenting styles not being recognized. Two-parent, heterosexual environments are assumed. In the Oedipus complex, Freud claimed that boys unconsciously fall in love with their mothers, so again all boys are assumed to be heterosexual. Any who grow to be homosexual develop this way because of an unresolved Oedipus complex, which was deemed to be abnormal. Not only does this imply that homosexuality is inferior, but it also ignored the possibility of female homosexuality altogether. While Freud's theories continue to be influential, they must be recognized as being a product of the era in which they were devised.

Gender bias in psychological research is a historic problem that results from the dominance of men in science during the formative years of psychology as a discipline. Because this book covers major historical theories and research in psychology, it is guilty, much like many other similar texts, of presenting ideas mostly developed by men, using males as subjects in their research. As a result, a lot of what we know about human psychology may not be applicable to women.

Fortunately, according to the American Psychological Association's Center for Psychology Workforce Analysis, the percentage of women receiving or studying for PhDs in psychology has risen from 20 per cent in 1970 to nearly 72 per cent in 2005. However, we must still be mindful that many of the approaches and theories that form the foundations of psychology were dominated by male, Western, industrialized ideals and represent the values of the era in which they were devised.

Index

Picture credits

Alamy: 20, 46, 48, 52, 71, 72, 84, 87, 101, 122, 144, 159, 162, 171, 174, 188, 190, 218, 231, 236.

Emily Ralls: 29, 101, 99.

Getty: 189, 203, 227, 232, 239, 247, 249.

Public domain: 21, 23, 58, 129, 131, 137, 222, 227, 143.

Shutterstock: 9, 11, 13, 15, 18, 19, 24, 25, 26, 28, 29, 31, 32, 34, 38, 39, 42, 42, 46, 54, 55, 59, 60, 62, 64, 76, 79, 85, 88, 91, 94, 96, 98, 100, 103, 105, 105, 105, 108, 109, 110, 112, 125, 128, 133, 140, 149, 153, 154, 156, 158, 163, 164, 176, 184, 193, 198, 201, 207, 208, 210, 214, 218, 219, 220, 225, 243.